The Silverlake Project

THE SILVERLAKE PROJECT

Transformation at IBM

ROY A. BAUER
EMILIO COLLAR
VICTOR TANG
with
JERRY WIND
PATRICK HOUSTON

New York   Oxford
OXFORD UNIVERSITY PRESS
1992

Oxford University Press

Oxford   New York   Toronto
Delhi   Bombay   Calcutta   Madras   Karachi
Petaling Jaya   Singapore   Hong Kong   Tokyo
Nairobi   Dar es Salaam   Cape Town
Melbourne   Auckland

and associated companies in
Berlin   Ibadan

Copyright © 1992 by Oxford University Press, Inc.

Published by Oxford University Press, Inc.
200 Madison Avenue, New York, New York 10016

Oxford is a registered trademark of Oxford University Press

Library of Congress Cataloging-in-Publication Data
Bauer, Roy A.
The Silverlake project : transformation at IBM /
Roy A. Bauer, Emilio Collar, Victor Tang
with Jerry Wind, Patrick Houston.
p.   cm.   Includes bibliographical references and index.
ISBN 0-19-506754-1
1. International Business Machines Corporation.
2. Computer industry—United States—Management—Case studies.
3. IBM AS/400 (Computer)
I. Collar, Emilio.   II. Tang, Victor.   III. Title.
HD9696.C64I483135   1992
338.7′61004′0973—dc20   91-32337

2 4 6 8 9 7 5 3 1

Printed in the United States of America
on acid-free paper

This book is dedicated to the people of IBM Rochester.
The success of the Silverlake
Project and the winning of the
Malcolm Baldrige National Quality Award
resulted from their hard work, their sacrifice,
and, most of all, their faith in themselves.

This book is also dedicated to our customers
and business partners for their loyalty and
assistance, without whom Silverlake would
have been very different.

Foreword

This is a remarkable tale. IBM had an amazing success with its AS/400 mid-range family of computers. So?

The "so" is revolution and transformation—fast, no less. Disarray is too kind a word for IBM's position in the growing, important mid-range computer business in 1986. Competitors were attacking from every point on the compass. A major project aimed at righting the ship was an expensive fiasco, and had to be canceled. Worse yet, the firm didn't even know how bad the damage was. Rising revenue effectively masked plummeting market share; and in fact, IBM Rochester didn't even know how to measure market share.

Twenty-eight months later, a relatively neglected development lab in Rochester, Minnesota was the talk of IBM. Two years later, the same group had added the prestigious Baldrige quality prize to impressive gains in market share and profitability.

The enormity of the shift is hard to overstate. (Tally the revenue the group generates and you'd have the world's second largest computer company—behind IBM, of course.) A $1 billion development project engaged thousands of engineers in building a hopelessly complicated, 10-million-part machine. Production took place at 37 sites on three continents. The AS/400 was launched globally—in 27 different languages and with 2,500 applications software programs. And it all had to be done—for survival's sake—in two years instead of the normal four!

Complexity is only one dimension of the magnitude of the task. It's no exaggeration to say that *everything* about the way IBM managed at Rochester was set on its ear by the Silverlake gang and their associates.

It began rather innocently. A five-person skunk works demonstrated the validity of the Silverlake approach and cobbled together a prototype in record time. But that was the least of it.

Next, a massive reorganization got the huge Rochester group focused. ("Focus" is one of three authors'—each intimately involved in the project—favorite words.) Attacking cycle-time waste—by complete reconception of the development and manufacturing processes—was earth-shattering, too, turning decades of IBM (and industry) practice on its ear.

None of these structural shifts, significant as they were, would have mattered a whit if the Rochester team hadn't been determined to bring the overused e-word, empowerment, to life for line operatives and senior technical people alike. (They even managed, virtually overnight, to increase the flow of top-drawer technical initiatives, by halving the time and hassle it took to file a patent application.)

But perhaps the most exciting initiatives were in service to the customer. New Rochester development lab boss Tom Furey struck at the core of IBM's mid-range woes from the start by asking: "Who are our customers?" "What do they want?"

"Incredible as it may sound," Bauer, Collar, and Tang write, "no one at IBM Rochester could adequately answer these two...questions." Thus, a 9 percent mid-range computer market share (down from about 33 percent a few years earlier) actually turned out to be even worse than it sounded: a 15 percent share where one-quarter of the demand was generated (among IBM's traditional big customers) and a paltry 6 percent share where three-quarters of the demand—and future potential—resided (mid-size customers and establishments). Needless to say, such findings fundamentally reshaped the project.

(There's lots more, of course. Hardware-oriented IBM wrenched its attention to application software to support targeted business segments. The secrecy-obsessed firm moved heaven and earth to turn "outsiders"—customers, distributors, vendors—into "insiders," almost from the start of the project. And the product launch process was completely reconceived to deal with past customer-perception problems.)

But maybe I've *still* bypassed the key element. In response to Furey's demands, the authors say "we began acting like a business" rather than a series of arrogant, warring functional tribes. "Acting like a coherent business" may be the largest challenge for moderate-sized bits of large organizations in tomorrow's tumultuous business environment.

There are lessons in these pages for almost all firms of all sizes. Above all, we are reminded that such an effort must be encompassing. Each part of this saga (the book is organized around 10 management principles) is exciting and holds vital lessons. But like it or not, this is pretty much a story of "do all 10 or else." That is, each part reinforced the others—and the overall result simply could not have been achieved without the transformation that took place in *every* nook and cranny of the business.

The best news is that the authors don't skimp on the details. This is not a recipe book. Yet it does constitute a blow-by-blow account—warts and all—of two extraordinary years in the life of a large-scale business revival.

IBM says it has 50,000 competitors—the Silverlake team discovered 250 major competitors in their bailiwick alone. The competitor/competitiveness explosion may be a little bit greater in information technology than in other industries, but not by much. The fact is that such sweeping turnabouts in management practice are musts for any would-be survivor.

Hats off to the IBM Rochester for what they achieved—*and* for telling us about it. (The telling per se is a big step down the path to revitalization for beleaguered IBM.) I'm pleased to be asked to "stand beside them" via this foreword.

Tom Peters
The Tom Peters Group

Preface

This book tells the inside story of the making and marketing of an extraordinarily successful new computer. At an operation in Rochester, Minnesota—literally in the midst of some cornfields—a machine, code-named the Silverlake, was born. It became one of the best-selling computers ever created by the International Business Machines Corporation, a feat all the more notable because IBM is one of the world's biggest and oldest computer companies and the maker of everything from small personal computers to giant mainframes.

But this book isn't really "about" the making of computers. Nor is it really "about" IBM. It transcends those strictures and goes to a level far more universal. This is really a book about how a small group of people in a distant part of a giant corporation transformed themselves—transformed themselves into a market-driven team that became a model for others to follow. It's also about the principles of management that guided their metamorphosis and their eventual rise to a premier place not only within IBM but within the whole of American business.

In this sense, the story of the Silverlake is a parable. Against the grand backdrop of modern commerce, it's a small tale but one that illustrates bigger and broader lessons—lessons useful to almost *any* organization facing the ever more arduous demands of existing, let alone thriving, in the often roiling global marketplace. The authors believe that Silverlake's lessons can be applied to any organization that must change to be globally competitive. And, unlike many of today's most popularized management techniques, these lessons do not owe their origins to foreign countries. They were made in the U.S.A. and emerged from a long American heritage for management innovation and advancement. They were honed for modern circumstances through good old Yankee ingenuity and common sense.

But this isn't just another business "how-to" book. Four things set it apart. The first is that it shows how certain management practices *were instilled in a real-life enterprise competing in global markets*. Second, it explains how they were applied *from the beginning of that enterprise all the way to the end*. Third, it describes how the practices came together *to make for an all-encompassing approach to a business endeavor*. Fourth, it *frankly addresses the problems encountered all along the way*. In other words, this is not a book about theory—it's one about reality.

The authors decided to write this book in the same way that the Rochester team approached the Silverlake Project. They responded to market demand. At the 16th International Research Seminar in Marketing at La Londe les Maures, France, in the summer of 1989, the authors made a presentation about the Silverlake story and the basic management concepts that emerged. The audience of business executives, university professors, and other researchers—coming together from North America, Europe, and Asia—reacted by demanding to know more. Similar responses to presentations made by the authors at government agencies, other corporations, and prestigious business schools left no doubt: The Silverlake story needed to be put into a more enduring form.

A word about the authors' voice as it emerges in the book. When the pronoun "we" appears, it refers to the whole Silverlake team. It never means only Bauer, Collar, and Tang. Inevitably, however, the authors, each of whom played a major role at Rochester, appear at times in the story. When they do, they are described in the third person—as though speaking of a colleague. This was done in the cause of objectivity and accuracy. Although it may at first seem jarring, we hope that the reader will quickly become accustomed to the convention.

The authors resorted to a second convention too. In each

chapter, the first reference to any of the 10 Silverlake management principles is highlighted in italic type. This was done to emphasize the sustained and interwoven role they played throughout the Silverlake Project.

Like the Silverlake Project itself, this book was a team effort. Roy A. Bauer, Emilio Collar, and Victor Tang were members of the Silverlake team. They lived the story told here. This book reflects their recollections and their own particular perspective on events and, occasionally, broader business issues. Others may have seen it differently from their vantage points. But the authors tried to remain as honest as possible to events and efforts that they were intimately involved in helping to initiate and implement.

The authors also wish to recognize Dr. Jerry Wind, Professor of Marketing at the University of Pennsylvania's Wharton School. He worked as a consultant to the Silverlake Project and helped with the management principles to which the project owed so much of its success.

Patrick Houston took the authors' draft of the Silverlake story and through hours of interviews and talks helped them clarify the relationship between the story and the management principles. Most of all, though, he transformed the result into a cogent and compelling narrative. In its way, this transformation was as important to this endeavor as the transformation of the Rochester team was for the Silverlake computer.

Rochester, Minn.　　　　　　　　　　　　　　　R.A.B.
August 1991　　　　　　　　　　　　　　　　　E.C.
　　　　　　　　　　　　　　　　　　　　　　　V.T.

Acknowledgments

The authors owe a deep debt to these executives who made a real difference in our work and in Silverlake. Tom Furey, our leader and mentor, who gave us the opportunity to participate and learn. He imparted the vision that made organizational transformation possible and steered the course that allowed Silverlake to become a reality. Steve Schwartz whose leadership and empowering style permitted the metamorphosis of IBM Rochester. George Conrades who gave IBM Rochester confidence and energy by his faith in our product line and conviction that Rochester could do it. Bill Grabe consistently broke new ground in marketing, and by personal example taught us the meaning of crossfunctional teamwork and executive decisiveness. Bob LaBant encouraged us in our work. He is proving that no matter how excellent a business is, it can be better through continuous improvement and innovation.

Silverlake was a team effort; the authors acknowledge the following executives for their assistance. Jim Coraza, for his steady and stabilizing systems management. Dave Schleicher, for his unselfish dedication and the unprecedented effort by his programming team. Larry Osterwise, for his leadership in manufacturing cycle time and site quality improvement. Debbie Miller, whose marketing insight and crisp unequivocating style was so instrumental in the development of a distinctive image for Silverlake. Al Cutaia, whose pioneering development with customers resulted in major innovations and new technology-intensive applications. Julie Furey, who communicated in such a compelling way the uses and benefits of Silverlake. Jim Flynn, for his drive, sacrifices, and engineering innovations. His untimely death is a loss to IBM Rochester and has left a void for all those who toil at the frontiers of computer engineering. His example and the fruits of his creativity, however, live on in every Silverlake computer produced by IBM Rochester.

Acknowledgments

The authors had the rare privilege of working with a unique team of professionals and managers whose commitment to Silverlake, drive for excellence, and ability to innovate turned our work into high adventure. They could have played it safe, but chose our untravelled road—full of risk, ambiguity, and intellectual challenge. We are especially grateful to Dave Arrindell, Terry Bird, Ralph Clark, Bob Cooper, Ted Dunnington, Bob Dunseath, Gary Etter, Gerry Falkowski, Pete Hansen, John Henry, Bruce Jawer, Tom Konakowitz, Maggie McNally, Mark McNeilly, Dan Mersel, Diane Miller, Don Mitchell, Jack Scheetz, Paul Strand, Bill Schneiderman, Jorge Vizcaino, and Bob Weir. They made our job easy and fun.

Silverlake was a high-risk project; our days were filled with crises and panic situations. In that environment, the authors quickly learned the difference our patient and efficient secretaries made to us and our organizations. Sandy Benfield, Barb Berry, and Dawn Durst are the best.

There were many people in Rochester who contributed to the Malcolm Baldrige self assessments. The "swat" team of Kevin Andersen, Dale Goodfriend, Lori Kirkland, Greg Lea, and Rick Linder deserve special mention. Without this team's hard work, dedication, loyalty, and commitment to excellence, we would not have won the Malcolm Baldrige Award. Jerry Graf, Gordy Hall, Bill Fuhrman, and the rest of the IBM Rochester publications staff deserve special mention for their dedication, attention to detail, and creativity in support of quality and the Malcolm Baldrige Award.

We thank our families. Although neglected during the Silverlake project, ignored during the writing of this book, and overlooked during the Baldrige submission, they encouraged us to persevere and were unfailing in their support. Special thanks to Liz Bauer, Luisa Collar, Cheryl Houston, and Wendy Tang for their patience and support during the writing of this book.

Thanks to Herb Addison, our editor at Oxford, for his keen judgments and sure hand in guiding this book to its final form. And to Mary Sutherland, also from Oxford, for her efficient project management.

Contents

The Silverlake Project

1

CORPORATE TRANSFORMATION IN A CORNFIELD

We are falling off the cliff and don't even know it.

—JACK BELL, Program Manager, Application Business Systems Headquarters

How could we possibly make a difference? Especially from out here? As far as anyone else was concerned we were just hicks. We were as far removed from the power centers of corporate America as you could get and still remain in the continental United States.

This reality confronted us every day, even as we drove to work. Right across the road from the main entrance and a sweep of high-tufted prairie grass, we passed a little clutch of structures—the white clapboard house, a windmill, an out building, and a barn—that were part of the old Rabehl farm. A few hundred yards straight ahead, unfurling over the gentle hills, we could watch the progress of the local corn crop—stubbly green in spring, knee-high by July, papery pale in late fall.

3

We were stuck out in a locale more akin to combines, county fairs, and the fall harvest than to computers, corporate meetings, and annual sales and profits. In fact, if there was anything—anything at all—serving as an appropriately symbolic backdrop for what we did and what we had to say, it was that our out-of-the-way part of the country is about a geography in transition. We lived and worked on the margins of the Midwestern prairie, where the North woods give way to the bluffs of the Mississippi River valley and then to the lush, flat farmlands of the plains. If the landscape was about change, so were we. We transformed ourselves. In the process, we not only saved our jobs by creating one of the best-selling mid-range computers— ever—we went on to win the most prestigious award in American business today, the much coveted Malcolm Baldrige National Quality Award.

And the sweet irony is that, though we may be out in the cornfields, people listen to us. We make a difference.

We have become an exemplar to our company, the International Business Machines Corporation, one of the biggest and most prestigious organizations in the world. Not only that, but after winning the Baldrige, hundreds of companies began sending delegations of representatives out into the cornfields to hear what we had to say. They wanted to learn our story, even if it meant trudging to the hinterlands.

This is our story—how we made and marketed an extraordinarily successful computer code-named Silverlake. We see it as a parable, a small tale that conveys a much larger lesson. In fact, much of what happened to us during the 1980s was at least symbolic, if not outright symptomatic. Many of the problems we faced are the same ones legions of other companies competing in the global marketplace continue to wrestle with today. We overcame our problems, and we like to think that the lessons we learned along the way can help other companies and enterprises.

We are IBM Rochester, a computer development and manufacturing operation in Rochester, Minnesota, a city of 70,000. Even in our pastoral setting, surrounded on three sides by croplands, there's no mistaking our true colors as a

4

corporate entity. All you have to do is stand back and take a good look at our sprawling operations, which cover an area equal to 75 football fields. The main group of interlocking, two-story buildings has smooth glass and steel-panel walls separated by aluminum mullions, making them look as if they're dressed in that most corporate of corporate uniforms, the pinstripe suit. The building is a deep blue—the trademark IBM blue.

IBM came to Rochester in 1956 when the company purchased 401 acres of land occupied by the Allen, Cassidy, and Clark family farmsteads. IBM's arrival marked one of the three most important events in Rochester's history since its founding in the 1850s by New England farmers. The first was the 1883 tornado that killed 23 townsfolk. And the second was the creation not long afterward of what became the world-renowned Mayo Clinic. Indeed, when IBM President Thomas Watson, Jr., the son of IBM's founding father, came to Rochester to announce the company's plan to build a plant, the *Rochester Post-Bulletin* called it "the greatest thing for the city since the founding of the Mayo."

We started off making readers for the punch cards now a relic to bygone days of the Computer Age. We worked hard. We grew. Soon we became the site of an IBM "development laboratory" where engineers and programmers began designing and building new computers. We hatched a successful line of computers for small to medium-sized businesses. We manufactured these computers here too.

Despite the steady stream of well-received computers we turned out, we toiled in relative obscurity. Even though we mounted sales in the billions of dollars, we still only contributed a fraction to IBM's mammoth overall revenues, and were way down the list when it came to comparing us as revenue producers to its other computer lines, such as mainframes. So, to IBM, we were a nice little business. We were out of sight and out of mind. They left us alone and we kept to ourselves. We met our sales and profit goals year after year.

In the early 1980s, we started to get more attention, though. Unfortunately, it was for a reason we hardly relish-

5

ed. We were in trouble. Deep trouble.

We had been losing market share—at a rapid clip—to a growing number of aggressive competitors. What's more, our existing product line was moving rapidly toward obsolescence; our customers were simply outgrowing it. And because an effort to create a breakthrough replacement computer ended in failure, we had nothing—not even on the drawing boards—in the works to replenish our aging line of offerings.

We were convinced our very existence was in jeopardy. In a desperate attempt to save ourselves, we set out to design and build a new computer. It was the Silverlake, named after a downtown Rochester landmark. And it was a long shot. The odds against us were 1,000 to one since we had just two years to complete the project—*less than half the time it normally took to bring a new computer to market.*

Midway through 1988, however, our fortunes changed. Completely. We had our new computer, formally known as the IBM AS/400. Within months of its introduction, it had become one of IBM's most successful new products. And we became a consistent IBM bright spot. From the time of its introduction right through a national recession in 1990, sales of the AS/400 grew at double-digit annual rates. Had we been on our own, our revenues would have been enough to make us the second biggest computer maker in the United States, behind IBM itself. Best of all, we began reclaiming market share. We were no longer a nice little business out on the prairie. We were a nice *big* business.

We did even better than that. In 1990, we took a place at the pinnacle of IBM, one, in fact, at the apogee of American business: IBM Rochester won the Malcolm Baldrige National Quality Award. While the award went to IBM Rochester as a whole, many of the accomplishments that figured into our Baldrige-winning performance traced their origins back to the Silverlake Project. In winning the Baldrige, we elevated ourselves to exemplar. We became the epitome of corporate transformation and renewal being held up before all of IBM, which by then was well into its own efforts to reverse its own overall market share slide.

How did we do it? What was behind our transfiguration? The first thing we did was embrace a different philosophy toward business. One of our problems was that we had become a *product-driven* enterprise. Our computers—the machines themselves—became everything to us. We cared more about pleasing our own purist ambitions for technology than about whether our machine actually did what its users—our customers—wanted.

We'd forgotten how to do something we'd always done so well before. We didn't listen to our customers. When it became clear that our selfish neglect was at the root of our market-share slide, we vowed to change. We decided to recast IBM Rochester as a *market-driven* enterprise. And what is that? A market-driven enterprise makes reaching and serving its markets its main concern. That certainly means matching and surpassing the competition. It also means reacting swiftly to economic conditions—the ups and downs. And it involves responding to the opportunities that chance and innovation often create.

But most of all, it means putting the customer above everything else. The market-driven enterprise's paramount concern is anticipating and then meeting—no, exceeding—customer expectations. When you meet and exceed what a customer expects, you sell. You also nurture loyalty, so you sell more. Delighted customers tout your product for you—and with a credibility that no amount of marketing and advertising can buy. You sell still more. When you sell, revenues grow. Since customers buy more products that delight them with pleasant surprises, profits rise. And there, in a nutshell, you have it: Success.

The other virtue of the market-driven philosophy is that it takes into account virtually every one of the elements that figure into business success. Too many enterprises assume that all you have to do is develop a product and get it to the market. If you're advanced enough, experienced enough, efficient enough, or dominant enough, the thing will simply sell itself.

That's the way we saw it: We created computers. For decades no one was better and we knew what it took. So we

7

designed and developed machines based on *our* expectations. But then we essentially started making machines for
ourselves, not our customers. Once we were ready with a
new machine, it's not oversimplifying to say that we just
turned our creation over to sales, boasting, "Here, this
machine is perfect in every way. It's going to sell itself.
Customers will love it. After all, we do." But, unfortunately,
we weren't the ones using the machine in the ways real customers did in real businesses in the real world outside IBM
Rochester.

In most businesses, success demands more than an
excellent product. A market-driven enterprise, by the very
nature of its approach, realizes this. By becoming beholden
to its markets, a market-driven company takes into account
competition, economic conditions, and unforeseen opportunities. It selects only certain markets—those in which it can
compete most effectively. It is focused; it has a clear sense
of itself and realizes, exactly, what business it can and
should be in, without going off on tangents. It analyzes
markets in an effort to discern what customers need and
want.

More than anything, a market-driven enterprise sees
that customers' needs extend beyond the product itself. In
our own case, we came to realize that customers wanted
more than just a computer. Their foremost concern was to
run and grow their business. To do that, they required a
computer—the machine itself—yes. But when it came to
data-processing, they needed more. They demanded a
broader solution. And that broader solution included providing them with applications software and an adequate
sales, support, and service network.

Along the way to transforming the IBM Rochester development laboratory into a market-driven organization, we
were also shaping it—and running it—as an enterprise
more akin to a real business. Before this change, the lab
was a place where new computers were designed and built,
without giving any account to much else. But as a market-
driven entity we began acting like a *business*—with all the
requisite concerns and disciplines. We began to pay more

8

and more attention not just to technology but to planning, finance, sales and marketing, support and service, and, most of all, to customer needs—in other words, to *all* the factors it takes to be a bona-fide success in today's business world.

While getting the Silverlake to market in half the normal time, we were forced to launch several initiatives that broke new ground. At that point, we were simply doing what had to be done. Only after the fact were we finally able to distill what we did into its essence. Now, we can say that our success boiled down to 10 management principles.

These principles have wide applicability, and not just to commercial businesses. Even nonprofit enterprises and government agencies may find them helpful. A few are new and innovative; most are tried and true. What we have to offer, more than anything else, is not so much a textbook treatment of each one, but an illustration of how they worked—not in theory but in reality. The Silverlake Project is really a case study. It shows how these principles came to bear on an enterprise *from beginning to end*. What's more, it demonstrates how they interplayed and rested on each other. If the Silverlake was a success, it was because these principles were applied not piecemeal but *in an all-encompassing way*.

The 10 Silverlake principles of general management to emerge from our success are:

- **Appoint a leader with vision.** A leader is different from a manager. Managers plan, budget, organize, and control. Leaders transform and renew. They see ahead to possibilities others don't. From this they articulate a vision—a picture, painted in broad strokes, of what the organization ought to be and where it should go. Leaders bring their vision to fruition by liberating the creative energies of those in an organization. And they inspire people to perform beyond their capabilities.

- **Institutionalize that vision by picking the right people and giving them the right mission.** Leaders

9

build organizations that carry on even after they're gone. They do so by creating organizational structures that reflect the enterprise's visions, its values, and, most of all, its *business goals and objectives*. Then they staff those structures with able, independent people. Once they put the right people in the right place and give them a clearly defined mission, they get out of the way, trusting their people and the organization to make good on what must be done.

- **Empower your people.** People move organizations. To get power, you must give *them* power. If they are to have the power to do their jobs, they must have two things —authority and resources. Trust them to use their own good judgment and give them the leeway to do so. And since workers are only as good as their tools, they must be properly equipped. In today's modern workplace that means supplying them with skills, knowledge, and up-to-date technology. Empowerment also means exciting people—revving them up through the use of inspiration and rewards.

- **Use cross-functional work teams.** Gone are the days when each of the functional entities of an organization —planning, development, manufacturing, sales, service —could operate as fiefdoms unto themselves. In today's complex world, each and every function plays an integral role; each brings its own unique and essential perspective. No matter how unrelated those views may sometimes seem, almost any endeavor you undertake will suffer when you ignore any one of them. To tap those insights and experiences, form partnerships involving functions from across the enterprise. Tackle problems or projects by forming groups of people that criss-cross the organization.

- **Segment your market, choose the appropriate segments, and position your product within those segments.** Markets can be broken down into sub-markets.

Once a market is segmented, pick those on which to focus your resources. All this should be done systematically. Once you've selected your target markets, position your product in a way that differentiates it from the competition. This usually comes down to articulating its features and benefits *as seen through the eyes of the customer*.

- **Research and model your markets and business.** Business may still be an art. But it's at least as much a science. It's not good enough anymore to rely on anecdotal experiences and judgments. Systematic approaches must be used. These include methodologies, tools, and models for gathering data, analyzing it, and shaping it in a way that allows you to simulate developments and predict outcomes. Research and modeling are crucial to transforming raw data into meaningful knowledge.

- **Allocate resources by setting priorities.** It's a rare organization that has unlimited resources. Nearly every company these days finds itself trying to do more with less. Making tradeoffs is inevitable. If one thing gets funding, another won't. The best way to make those tradeoffs is to establish priorities based on organizational goals and objectives. State your goals. Rank objectives. Rank markets. Rank investments. Do it systematically—and do it knowing that a number of different factors will figure into it. Most important, do it with the entire organization's overarching interests in mind.

- **Break time barriers by using parallel processes and getting it right the first time.** Everything these days has to be done in less time. In fact, time—getting to market first or fastest—has actually become as crucial as anything else in the race for competitiveness. Reject the old sequential, step-by-step way of doing things. The various facets of any endeavor can be pursued concurrently, thus compressing the time to completion. Save time, too, by using an approach that insists on getting it

11

right from the beginning; instead of having to spend time removing defects after the fact, eliminate them during conception or design.

- **Form partnerships with outsiders, especially customers.** The world had become too complex. No one can do it completely on their own anymore—even the biggest companies don't have the resources to do everything in-house. Reach out for insights and expertise. Identify the key outside constituencies to your business—suppliers, distributors, customers, and others—and make them insiders to the extent that you can. Have them review and verify your plans. Tapping into the expertise of others saves time and resources and improves quality. At the very least, listen, and listen closely, to them.

- **Shape and continuously exceed your customers' expectations.** In today's unforgiving markets, a product's introduction to the marketplace is one of its most crucial junctures. But the introduction isn't a one-day event. It's a process. Start preparing well before introduction by addressing all the things that may affect your customers' perceptions and expectations. Once the product hits the market, stay on top of it. Do all that you can to make certain that your product continues to meet and exceed what the customer expects.

These object lessons formed the success of the Silverlake Project. And, make no mistake about it, this is a book about lessons. Most chapters have as their primary focus one of these principles; in many cases, the principles serve as sub-themes. But the order of presentation was determined by this book's other most notable feature—it's told as a story and as such takes a narrative form. So what you find in the following pages is a chronology, an inside account of the way it unfolded.

In trying to satisfy its dual roles as teacher and storyteller, the chapters sometimes overlap. Then again, the Silverlake Project unfolded in that way too. We learned as we went along and the process was less than orderly. Some-times, it felt as though we were trying to build a jetliner while it was in flight!

Nevertheless, the basic sequence of events remains intact. Our story has a beginning, a middle, and an ending. And in the beginning, we were near despair. We were in dire need of someone who could captain our sinking ship back to shore. We got that person in the form of a little-known IBM city slicker. He arrived in March 1986—in the face of our overwhelming dubiousness about his ability to rescue us before we all went down.

2

LEADERSHIP
AND
VISION

That's what we want to become.

— TOM FUREY, Director, IBM Rochester Development Laboratory

As 1985 came to a close, we needed the business equivalent of a Churchill—someone to see us through our darkest hour. Instead, they sent us Tom Furey. And we responded with a resounding, "Who?"

We needed a proven quantity, someone with a track record for turnaround. But Furey was an unknown, a great big question mark. He'd never been in charge of a major operation, let alone a rescue mission of our magnitude. At the very least, our situation called for a rising star, a name from among the few up-and-comers everybody recognized as headed for a place at the top. But Furey's name didn't reside on anyone's short list of heir apparents.

To top it off, he was an outsider, an IBM East Coast smoothie coming to the prairie. When he finally arrived in

March 1986, first impressions didn't make us feel any better. For all his inexperience, Furey came across with the almost imperious air of a chief executive officer. And he didn't exactly endear himself to us when, as one of his first acts, he decided to redecorate his office and an adjoining conference room because he thought it was too "spartan" for someone of his status.

Furey's arrival only intensified speculation about our darkening fate. We saw yet another signal that we were about to be written off. Why else would they have sent us a no-name like Tom Furey? Couldn't they see? Even if Furey actually was a competent executive, we needed more than that. We needed a *leader*.

At one time or another, every enterprise, large or small, requires a leader at the top—not just a manager. There's vast difference between the two, and an entire body of knowledge has grown up around the distinction. According to prevailing wisdom, a manager's job is more akin to an engineering task. By the definition taught in every basic business school class, managers plan, budget, organize, and control. They implement and execute. Unfortunately, during the post-World War II era when American business had its way in a world against little competition, the manager's job became largely custodial; managers made sure things just kept running smoothly.

But in the new age of global hypercompetitiveness, breakneck change, and electronic speed it's not enough for someone in charge to be a manager, no matter how professional. Companies need less management and more *leadership*. People want to be led, not managed.

A leader's brief is far more sweeping. A leader nurtures quantum change. Instead of moving an organization ahead in increments, a leader renews and transforms it. By the definition emerging from among academics and management consultants, a leader envisions possibilities that others don't. A leader articulates those insights into a *vision*, a clear and simple picture, a dream, really, and one unique to the organization that lays out what it can be or where it ought to go. A leader gets people to embrace the

15

vision by making it clear that it's doable but its realization hinges on their contribution. By example, by cheerleading, by recognition and rewards, and by generating pride, a leader inspires people to bring a vision to fruition. Leaders get ordinary people to do extraordinary things.

And in 1986, we needed a leader at IBM Rochester because we had to do some extraordinary things. If we didn't, our 30-year-old operation was destined for oblivion and we knew it. IBM was starting to take a hard look at its resources back then, and if it wanted a place to cut, consolidate, or close, its Rochester operation was a good candidate. We were in trouble. And to understand why requires a short trip back into our history.

IBM Rochester started out in 1956 as a small manufacturing facility. IBM built a plant in the rural Midwest for all the same reasons that other companies have satellite manufacturing facilities dotting the countryside: Real estate is cheaper, labor costs are lower, and the work ethic is strong. According to local legend, Rochester, a phlegmatic prairie town in southeastern Minnesota that had already achieved some degree of notoriety as home to the renowned Mayo Clinic, got the nod over other sites because IBM President Thomas J. Watson, Jr., had a World War II Army Air Force buddy from there. At the outset, IBM Rochester made components for computers, mostly the devices that punched, collated, and read those elongated do-not-bend-fold-or-mutilate cards that once served as the staple for processing computer data.

We got into computer manufacturing by happenstance. In 1966, a small group of our engineers designed a card reader that contained a processor; it had its own small computing capability. It wasn't much, but it made IBM Rochester home to enough electronics expertise so that, when IBM decided it wanted to make a computer for small to medium-size businesses, we were tapped for the job. Along with manufacturing, IBM created a "development laboratory" in Rochester—a staff of engineers and programmers to bring the new computer to life.

16

The lab gave birth to its first computer in 1969. It was the IBM System/3. True to its intended market, the System/3 embodied features that made it especially easy to use by smaller businesses. It employed a programming language so simple that a business didn't require a staff of professional programmers to create software for it. Eventually, many users didn't have to worry about creating their own software at all, because the System/3 offered a range of ready-to-use software applications for tasks such as manufacturing management, construction planning, scheduling, office administration, and more.

System/3 turned out to be a technological and business success. Attracted by its selection of ready-to-use software, businesses snapped it up. As the years rolled by, IBM Rochester generated a series of successor machines. It created the System/32 in 1975, the System/34 in 1977, and the System/36 in 1983, each one bringing new capabilities and more power to our business users. In 1976, IBM's development lab spawned the IBM 5100, an 80-pound "portable" computer. It was smaller than anything else on the market at the time and was a precursor to IBM's huge-selling Personal Computer.

Except for the 5100, these machines were all evolutionary descendants of the original System/3. But in 1978, IBM Rochester launched a new machine that made a leapfrog jump in technology and capability. It was the IBM System/38. It embodied advances that made programmers seven to 10 times more productive. And it contained, as standard features, a host of progressive new functions, including an integrated relational database, which made it possible to sort and categorize *all* the information stored inside, no matter what its form or source. Its technology was elegant—too elegant, perhaps. Many of its capabilities were too far ahead of their time to be understood and, therefore, fully appreciated by the market.

The System/38 had something else going against it: It was incompatible with the System/3 line; customers couldn't move all the software and data they'd created or bought for the System/34 over to the System/38. So the System/38 never achieved the popularity that the System/3 and its successors did. Nevertheless, because it represented such technical achievement, it drew a nearly zealous attachment from our most sophisticated users, not to mention the highbrow engineers and programmers who created it.

By the end of the 1970s, we were doing quite well for ourselves. We were productive; we turned out a steady stream of new products—a new or upgraded computer every two years. We delivered on time; schedules seldom slipped. We worked hard; our engineers and programmers often reported overtime exceeding the 40-hour work week by as much as 20 percent. Absenteeism was low. According to annual surveys IBM conducts among employees, morale was always at the highest levels among IBM's several development labs.

Along with developing and manufacturing computers, we made many items that went along with them—video-display terminals, storage disks, printers. For many years, we even had our own sales force. Instead of an operations site, we were more like a wholly owned subsidiary. Our autonomy bestowed on us our own unique culture.

Geography played a part too. For most IBMers, the plum assignments were at headquarters in Armonk, New York, the company's other Westchester County and East Coast locations, the West Coast, or overseas. People didn't exactly clamor to come to the frigid Upper Midwest. We responded to this slight with a stauncher brand of parochialism. It wasn't hard to be defensive. Many of us grew up in Minnesota and Wisconsin and other parts of the Midwest. Outsiders who came in seldom wanted to leave because Rochester is such a great place to raise a family. The result was that, in some circles of the corporation, we were considered provincial to the point of being distressingly aloof. They called us "Fortress Rochester," and we didn't raise a fuss about the characterization.

But if we were an outpost, we were a prosperous one. From the introduction of the System/3, sales just kept bounding. IBM doesn't release revenue figures for its operations sites, but, had we been on our own in 1980, our annual sales would have made us one of the nation's biggest computer companies, exceeded in size by IBM itself. Even at that, we were by no means a major contributor to IBM's colossal overall revenues. So we didn't get the attention that, say, our mainframe business did. Still, as far as we were concerned, IBM regarded us as nothing more than a nice little business—the top brass never had to worry about us. We were like the perfect child; we didn't cause any problems and we made our parents proud.

By the 1980s, however, all that began to change. Fortress Rochester started to come under siege. The mid-range market began undergoing explosive growth, and companies started rushing into it to claim part of the largess. As a result, competition converged from all sides. In the United States, Hewlett-Packard, Wang Laboratories, Data General, Tandem, and NCR began grabbing up market share by making computers used in business applications such as retailing, banking, and office administration. Startups such as Basic/4 and Prime entered the fray. And we found ourselves facing a growing number of competitors in our overseas markets too, including Italy's Olivetti, West Germany's Nixdorf, and Japan's Fujitsu.

But one of our stiffest challenges, at least in the United States, came from Digital Equipment Corporation of Maynard, Massachusetts. For a long time, DEC focused its machines in the market for scientific, engineering, and other technical applications. Emboldened by its success there, DEC moved in on our traditional turf—commercial businesses—and began making surprisingly strong inroads.

One of the main reasons DEC was able to do so well had to do with the issue of "compatibility." By the early 1980s, as computers began to suffuse every part of the workplace, many customers found themselves with a polyglot of machines—and a gold mine of data stashed in each. It became the ardent goal of many companies to have computers share data and work together. They wanted their mainframes, their mid-range machines, and their personal computers to operate together in a seamlessly integrated whole. But because of the idiosyncrasies of hardware and software on which different machines were based, they were incompatible; they couldn't share information or software. DEC, however, had a whole family of computers—its VAX line—that *were* compatible. DEC began pressing this advantage in the marketplace and snatching business away from us.

We were particularly vulnerable to the compatibility issue. The System/3 and its successors were incompatible with the System/38. What's more, other parts of IBM had come to the market with their own mid-range machines. Counting the System/36 and System/38, IBM had at least five mid-range computer lines. The others were the IBM 8100 used to distribute the processing and power of a mainframe out into departments and remote locations, the IBM/Series 1 for transaction processing (such as for automatic teller machines), and the IBM 4300 created to run applications used on IBM mainframes. None of these machines was compatible with each other; none could run the same applications software.

Having all these different machines confused our customers. If you wanted a mid-range computer from IBM, whom were you supposed to call? Customers often found themselves all the more befuddled by the visits they got from sales representatives from different parts of IBM —including those selling our machines—each one touting different computers as the best "single" solution to the same problem.

Having all these machines created internal problems for IBM too. To retain customers as they outgrow their machines—as they inevitably do—a computer maker must keep coming out with upgraded versions of existing machines or new ones altogether. But it takes heaps of money to design and develop a successor to a computer line. As the 1980s arrived, IBM realized it could no longer afford to sustain five separate computer lines. The bill was just too onerous.

So for the good of its customers—and its own good—IBM had no alternative but to address the issues of its incompatible and disparate mid-range computer lines. Its response was to hatch plans for a brand new machine—a machine it code-named Fort Knox.

The idea behind Fort Knox was straightforward. It was to serve as the single successor to IBM's diverse mid-range machines. Customers who owned different machines would be able to move their data and software onto a Fort Knox. While that sounds simple enough, making Fort Knox compatible with all those other machines posed a mind-boggling undertaking. If IBM made cars instead of computers, Fort Knox would have been tantamount to combining the features of a sports car, a station wagon, a compact, a luxury car, and a pickup truck into a single all-appealing vehicle.

The effort to build Fort Knox began in 1982. Because of its sheer magnitude, IBM took a different approach in developing it. Previously, the work of creating each of IBM's computers belonged to a single development lab. IBM Rochester gave birth to the System/36, and no one else got involved. But for Fort Knox, IBM parceled the work out among four different sites, with headquarters driving the entire undertaking. Eventually, the project involved some 4,000 people at Rochester and three other development labs. Work went on for about four years.

Then, in 1985, after investing millions of hours and hundreds of millions of dollars, IBM pulled the plug and killed Fort Knox. The concept proved unfeasible. Combining that many machines into one turned out to be a nightmare. And even though Fort Knox may have been technologically achievable, it became painfully evident that a machine with its capability would have had to carry a price tag far too high for its intended market of small to medium-sized users.

IBM's multi-site approach to creating Fort Knox played a role in its failure too. As it turned out, each site maintained a stubborn attachment to its own machines and its particular design approach. Perhaps because it's as much art as science, anyone who works on creating a new computer develops an emotional bond to it. So getting the engineers and programmers from all those different places to

21

come to some consensus was like getting Norman Mailer, John Updike, Tom Wolfe, and Gore Vidal—authors with their own unique styles—to write a single book together. It got so bad that people made jokes about it. "We really believe in multi-site development," one crack went. "We wish all our competitors would use it."

Even when headquarters was in agreement, the programmers and engineers working on Fort Knox often went home only to find what they'd agreed to do was impossible. When they reported back with their fruitless results, headquarters wouldn't hear of it. Unwilling to give ground on what precious little consensus it had forged, headquarters insisted they just keep plugging away. Delay followed delay.

The biggest problem was that IBM never got its troops to buy in to Fort Knox. Resistance mounted—and actually accelerated as Fort Knox looked more and more iffy. IBM Rochester may have been the pocket of stiffest opposition. A few among us had the temerity to come forth and criticize the project to top management. Some of those who did paid a price; they were dispatched from the project and sent on assignment to the equivalent of Siberia.

Along with the Fort Knox failure, we suffered two other setbacks in the early 1980s. IBM decided to designate our System/36 as *the* computer to challenge our competitors in the market for "office automation." The idea was to provide System/36 with the capability for handling a multitude of office tasks. But there was a problem. Over the years we had already taken the System/36 to the limits of its capability. When a computer approaches capacity, it slows down. Our System/36 for the office really huffed and puffed. In the end, we wound up providing the market with an uncompetitive package for performing office tasks.

The second reversal involved our beloved System/38. In 1984, with work still underway for Fort Knox, IBM publicly declared the System/38 "non-strategic." Because of Fort Knox, IBM no longer saw any need for the System/38. For all its advanced features, IBM considered the machine an anomaly. Implicit in its declaration was that IBM no longer intended to dedicate resources to upgrade or evolve the

22

System/38. The machine would simply be left to die on the vine. But when Fort Knox failed, the 20,000 customers who owned the machine found themselves facing a dead end. They had no place to grow or migrate.

The System/36 was at the end of its lifespan. System/38 had been given the kiss of death. Fort Knox was dead. We lost an entire product cycle—four years of work down the tubes with little to show for it. The upshot: By 1985, we didn't have a viable—let alone competitive—machine to offer. And because it typically took us four to five years to hatch a new machine, we were that far behind in our ever-intensifying battle with the competition.

Yet, we were even worse off—and didn't realize it. We were suffering from the "boiling frog syndrome." If you heat the water in which it sits, slowly, degree by degree, a frog will just remain there. Because the change is so gradual, the frog fails to sense the heat. It will simply remain in the water until it boils to death.

And so we sat. Our steadily rising revenues had obscured another gradual trend, one that put us into some very hot water. Even as sales went up in a growing market, the true measure of our performance—market share—had been going down. Our decline was nothing short of shocking. In the late 1970s, we claimed as much as a third of the global markets for mid-range computers. In 1985, when someone finally decided to check, it had shrunk to a measly single digit.

By 1985, we were really starting to sweat it. Or at least someone among us was, and, unlike the frog, he realized the time had come to leap. It was Pete Hansen, an experienced engineer and programmer at IBM Rochester.

A roly-poly figure, Hansen isn't exactly the image of the pinstriped "organization man." He is a consummate gear head, and can be seen tooling around Rochester in the hot rods he builds. Once a year he takes his souped-up snowmobile on a mad 10-day dash into the northernmost reaches of Minnesota's winter landscape. Hansen is also one of those proverbial straight-shooters; he says what he thinks, diplomacy and corporate politics be damned. He tried to convince IBM that Fort Knox wouldn't work. His prescience was rewarded by being removed from the project through a job promotion—one of those instances where "heads roll up."

Hansen is also one of those people we turned to when we had a problem and the chips were down. Hansen knew we had a problem and, to him, we faced only one option. We needed to create a new machine—and it had to be a hybrid of our own two most successful machines, the System/36 and the System/38. If we were to preserve our franchise, at least what was left of it, customers from both machines had to be able to migrate to the new one, which meant finding a way to make the incompatible System/36 and System/38 machines compatible with the new machine. The idea wasn't an original. We'd considered it before, but nothing came of the effort due mainly to a lack of communication and cooperation among the various constituencies at our site.

Hansen actually made a formal pitch to launch a project to create a new machine. His case went nowhere. However, he was not to be deterred. He went to Dave Schleicher, the head of programming for the IBM Rochester development lab, and got permission to set up his own "skunk works"—a small five-person project team that would go off on its own to explore the feasibility of creating a single successor to the System/36 and the System/38. Schleicher saw real possibilities in Hansen's proposal and gladly gave his assent.

Hansen picked four others for the mission: Larry Whitley, a System/36 engineer who was one of our foremost hardware designers; Tom Konakowitz, a product planner with an almost sixth sense for translating customer needs into product features; Wayne Richards, a reticent technologist with a far-reaching mind; and Erik Thorpe, another planner and a former IBM salesman who could peddle ice in Alaska.

The group represented a crucial mix of talents. Hansen knew software systems, Whitley knew hardware, Richards knew approaching technologies, Konakowitz knew customers, and, most important, Thorpe knew how to sell, an aptitude the team would dearly depend on when it came time to seek corporate support for its idea. None of them signed on to this maverick effort just because it was part of their job. They did it for deeper personal, even emotional, reasons. The demise of Fort Knox left a lot of people at IBM Rochester feeling as though they had something to prove, and Hansen's team members were among them.

At IBM, development projects always go by a code name. This is mostly for security reasons but also to build *esprit de corps*. For their effort, Hansen's group looked to a body of water. It was a lake formed out of the Zumbro River which meanders right through Rochester. The lake—it's more like a lagoon—doubles as a power-plant cooling reservoir. It also serves as the centerpiece of a picturesque city park, and, along with the water tower painted to look like an ear of corn, serves as one of Rochester's more unique landmarks.

Filled with heated water from the power plant, the reservoir never freezes, not even during Minnesota's famously frigid winters. As a result, some 25,000 Canada geese, rather than enduring the long flight south, remain content to make the lake their winter home and local residents see to it that the birds are well fed. The geese are a tourist attraction. Mayo Clinic doctors even prescribe the scene as a therapy for patients and their families.

This reservoir is known as Silver Lake. And it provided the code name for Hansen's project. The choice didn't have profound or even noble origins; that many geese leave a big mess. But the name *Silverlake* (Hansen's team contracted it to a single word) rolled off the tongue. It had a certain ring. And it conjured up images that associated nicely with the computer they had in mind—a shimmering, almost heavenly, work of creation.

Hansen's crew went to work on a prototype for Silverlake in the spring of 1985. Our desperation gave Hansen a certain mandate he didn't hesitate to assert. For example, when he requested a special piece of hardware, the engineering manager in charge said it would take three months. Hansen sat the man down and explained that he didn't have three months, and neither did *anyone* at IBM Rochester. *Everyone's* job was at stake, Hansen said, as he laid out the dire consequences of failure. If there were no engineers, he reminded the manager, there damn well wouldn't be much need for an engineering manager. Hansen had his hardware within a week.

By June, their work was showing real signs of promise. By then, they were receiving certain technical validations that reaffirmed their concept for a computer that could replace both the System/36 and the System/38. Within weeks Hansen's group had a working prototype. In this bare bones unit representing only a part of a full-scale machine, they had managed to prove the feasibility of their concept.

Nevertheless, as Hansen's group envisioned it, Silverlake would be an awesome technical undertaking; it was far bigger than anything we'd done before. For example, the System/38's operating system—its basic set of internal software instructions—consisted of less than 2 million lines of programming code. Silverlake's basic set of software instructions would take 7 million lines!

Technical issues aside, Silverlake confronted us with an even bigger challenge. After losing a product cycle to Fort Knox's demise, we realized that, in order to sustain a viable presence in the mid-range market, we needed a new machine by early 1988. We knew that our principal competitors would be coming out with upgraded or new machines by then. If we wanted to keep our customers from defecting, we had to have something new to offer too. But that meant cranking out a machine in two to three years—*or about half the time it normally took.*

In the ensuing months, Hansen's group began talking up the idea to others within the development lab, including planners, other engineers and programmers, and anyone else who would have to throw in on any such endeavor. They began making believers. In December 1985, they made a formal demonstration of their machine to senior managers of the IBM Rochester development lab. The team received a standing ovation. One manager enthused, "This is the breakthrough we've been waiting for for years!"

With our own IBM Rochester senior management now backing the idea, one more selling job yet remained. But it was the most crucial. IBM headquarters had to sign on to the idea. Early in 1986, Steve Schwartz, the executive in charge of our division, and our senior management team made a pitch to IBM's top executive management, including Chairman and CEO John Akers.

Hansen's prototype made it clear that the concept was most certainly workable. And then we laid out our ambitious timetable for bringing Silverlake into reality. And we told them what we thought it would cost—nearly $1 billion. In essence, we were asking IBM to make a billion-dollar bet on us. After deliberation, the word came down. IBM gave us a go. But, we heard, its approval didn't exactly amount to a vote of confidence. IBM's top brass called our cause a noble one, but they thought our timetable far too tight. Creating a new machine in two to three years was without precedent. But they did agree with us on one thing—when it came down to it, there was no alternative. If IBM wanted to preserve its base of System/36 and System/38 customers, if it wanted to maintain a viable presence in the mid-range market, the Silverlake was the company's only option.

This was the situation when Tom Furey arrived. The Silverlake was our only hope and we needed a leader to galvanize our efforts and bring the new machine to fruition. But was Furey really the one to do this? To the cynics among us, he was the result of the same backhanded conviction IBM was demonstrating to our cause; despite doubts that we could pull it off, there was just no other choice. Like the company's green light to Silverlake, his appointment, many of us thought, reflected resignation more than resolve.

Officially, Tom Furey came to us as director of our development lab, one of two sides to IBM Rochester. The other is a manufacturing operation, which, along with making computers, also produces data-storage devices. His new job put him in charge of 2,500 engineers and programmers involved in designing computer systems. And, of course, Silverlake became his to oversee.

Furey is a man with a disarmingly boyish face, which seemed somewhat at odds with his weight lifter's beefy build. When he arrived, he was, at 45, a 24-year veteran of IBM. Furey joined IBM fresh from college as a systems engineer, installing and programming IBM mainframe machines for customers in and around Albany, New York. From there, he became a software programmer at IBM's Kingston development lab and, eventually, one of its top software development managers. His technical contributions led to an appointment as an assistant analyzing new technologies under John Akers before Akers became IBM's chief executive officer.

Furey's nose for new technologies eventually put him in charge of a venture involving a large computer display screen—one four times bigger than a standard video display—that used a gas-plasma technology pioneered by IBM. But as a venture, the screen had a major problem: Its hefty cost kept customers at bay, and it was falling far short of the sales IBM had anticipated. Furey, however, found a way to deal with the dilemma. He pinpointed specialized uses among select customers, a tack that turned the enterprise into a viable business concern.

The appointment put Furey in charge not of a function but an entire business. He oversaw every aspect of the venture—engineering, manufacturing, planning, with profit and loss responsibility—just as though he was running his very own company.

This, more than anything, is what brought Furey to us. Furey was heading strategic planning for IBM's telecommunications product organization under Steve Schwartz, one of IBM's most seasoned executives known for his succinct mind, wide-ranging experiences, and his even wider-ranging business perspective. In 1985, Schwartz became head of the IBM business unit to which IBM Rochester belonged.

It was Schwartz who tapped Furey as our new lab director. He saw a manager with the technological wherewithal to head one of IBM's major development sites. But more than that, he pegged Furey as a manager who could think strategically and had the breadth, depth, and

the knack to run IBM Rochester's development lab as
though it were a *real business*, subject to the same disciplines as any other commercial enterprise.

In short, in Furey, Schwartz found a manager with the
right stuff to transform the lab into a *market-driven* enterprise. Schwartz sent Furey to us. And true to his trademark
management style, once he made the appointment, he got
out of Furey's way, trusting Furey to handle the lab
director's job as Furey saw fit.

Of course, we didn't view Furey as Schwartz did. To us,
Furey was a manager whose ascent was rapid, but not
meteoric. His career may have been well rounded, but, as
far as we could tell, Furey was in over his head. He'd never
been a lab director. He'd never been in charge of *any* major
enterprise at IBM. And he'd never headed anything as big
as our lab—certainly, nothing of Silverlake's magnitude.
This was the guy who was supposed to not only rescue our
jobs but IBM's entire stake in the mid-range market? As far
as we were concerned, there was no way—no way at all.

Like it or not, Furey became our new boss. And as any
executive new to an assignment, the first thing Furey
wanted to do was learn as much as he could about us. He
asked questions. How many customers do we have? Where
are they located? How many in the United States? How
many overseas? What models do they own? How old are the
computers they have? But instead of getting trenchant
answers from us, he got a lot of blank stares. Or anecdotes.

Furey wanted to know everything about us *as a
business*. But we never bothered ourselves too much with
all that. We were a development lab; our task was to
design, build, and program computers. It was beyond our
brief to address business issues or worry about things like
market share, or customers, or exhaustive market analyses.
Those were concerns that belonged to someone else. But
Furey saw it differently. To him, we most certainly were a
business, and we had damn well start acting that way.

Since we didn't have the answers, Furey decided we
were going to get them. To do that, he formed a *cross-
functional* task force, consisting of people from manufac-

turing, the development lab, and marketing. Between those three functions he figured, we'd certainly be able to come up with a credible profile of our existing business. To head the task force he picked Bill Harreld, a longtime IBM Rochester hand and a former manufacturing manager with a pit-bull mentality toward any project he took on; he just wouldn't let go until he vanquished it. Harreld and his task force spent six weeks compiling information. They sifted through records we kept on all our customers, both in the United States and abroad. They sorted through sales records. They scoured financial data. All this information was available in our own records, but no one had ever assembled it.

When the task force brought its *research* together, we began to realize some startling things about ourselves. We had more than 220,000 customers worldwide. Sixty percent of them existed outside the United States. We sold almost as many System/38 computers in Japan as we did in the United States. There was a huge infrastructure of independent software producers and other support services that had grown up around our computers. There were even magazines—published independently of IBM—dedicated solely to covering issues and developments about our computers.

As these and other findings began to cross Furey's desk, he started coming to some revelations of his own. Up to this time, Furey himself probably thought of IBM Rochester as a career way station. He had even admitted to some of us that coming to Minnesota wasn't exactly an assignment he coveted. But now Furey was beginning to see something about IBM Rochester that many of us didn't, something that IBM itself didn't either. Furey, a voracious reader, had begun encountering a steady stream of articles about the economic integration of Europe, the emergence of "Fortress Europe" as a huge, single market. American companies were busily planning how they might get a foothold there. We already had one. For years, he's been reading about how the Japanese had been beating up on U.S. companies in one industry after another. Yet we were winning in Japan's own back yard.

Furey was coming to a *vision*. As he saw it, IBM had in us a prize franchise. While most businesses were still aspiring to become global players, we'd already established ourselves. Given that, our potential was huge. Furey excitedly began telling people close to him that IBM Rochester, if it played its cards right, actually had the right stuff to become *the undisputed leader of the global mid-range market*. Instead of being a nice little business for IBM, we could become one of the major factors in the corporation's vast portfolio of businesses. As Furey saw it, Silverlake was the key, but it was also only the start. To us, Silverlake was going to be just another successor machine. If we just breathed a little harder and got it to the market on time, it would provide us with an incremental bump in growth —enough, we hoped, to save ourselves. But to Furey, Silverlake wasn't just another computer. It was a breakthrough product. And it was going to take us—all of us—to the top of IBM and to the heights of our industry segment.

At this early stage, Furey's vision seemed more like an apparition, wispy and indistinct around the edges. Later, we would realize that is the way a vision often gets its start. In many cases, the leader who has a vision does not come to it as an entirely rational act, nor as the fruit of conscious logic. It emerges from instinct or intuition in the form of a fuzzy outline. At the time, it just *felt* like the right thing to do. He saw the future, and he got his insights before he applied systematic reasoning to it.

As time went on, Furey's vision began to get more and more concrete. As it solidified, it became clear to him that he wanted to do two things.

First, he wanted to make IBM Rochester the industry leader in the mid-range market. To do that he had to build Silverlake in the unheard time frame of two to three years. Not only that but he had to deliver a machine that would wow customers, one that would set a new standard for the industry. And no matter how good it was, Silverlake alone wouldn't be enough. If we were going to rise to the top, we had to look beyond Silverlake—to its successor and the one after that. We had to be thinking way ahead to the new

31

technologies and features that would lead our customers well into the future. And that meant we needed a *long-term and overarching business strategy*. We needed to marshal our resources for this long haul. And we couldn't forget that our long-term viability depended on a foundation of rock-solid financial performance. We had to make money, and the more the better.

Second, he wanted to make IBM Rochester into an emblem for all of IBM. Furey's vision was to fashion IBM Rochester into *the* corporate exemplar of the market-driven enterprise. In 1986, IBM chairman John Akers was already sending the first signals of his intention to remold IBM into a market-driven company. Although IBM had always been a guarded, highly secretive organization, Akers took the unprecedented step that year of inviting customers to the company's top internal strategic planning conference.

Furey took note. At the time, Furey saw two possibilities for us. We could become a profit-driven enterprise, as most businesses are. But he felt that putting profits as our foremost goal placed too much emphasis on short-term results; it fostered shortsighted thinking. No, he figured it far better in the long run to make the customer our *raison d'être*. As Akers would later say, if we made customer satisfaction our goal, everything else, including profits, would follow. And by anticipating customer needs, IBM Rochester would find itself in an ongoing state of self-renewal.

To become a paradigm of the market-driven enterprise, we had to be more responsive to our customers. To become more responsive, we needed to look outward to our markets more, not inward to self-concerns. That meant managing by information, facts, and computer *modeling*; planning, market research, and forecasting must be disciplines on par with engineering and programming. To be more responsive, we had to coordinate our efforts more efficiently. We also needed the synergies of teamwork, a cross-functional approach that brought together the experience and talents of people from engineering, programming, planning, manufacturing, and marketing.

If we were going to be more responsive, we had to put

decision-making power in the hands of those who could act fast—those on the job, not those at the top of some grinding bureaucracy. And if they were going to handle this responsibility, we had to nurture their skills and talents. We had to *empower* them. If we were going to depend on them so much, we needed their hearts and minds too. If we were to be responsive to customer needs, we had to introduce new products ever more frequently. To get new products to the market more quickly we needed to *form partnerships* with outsiders.

Thus was Furey's vision. Having firmed it up, Furey set out to not only communicate it but to *sell* it. So he called us together in the company cafeteria. IBM Rochester is a austere place for the most part; you'll find worn linoleum more often than plush carpeting. And its layout is such that it has an almost maze-like quality. Its thin corridors always seem to be filled with a rush of people heading hither and yon into its warrens of tiny offices. The cafeteria, a cavernous room under a towering ceiling, is the biggest gathering place in our sprawling facility, resembling a fieldhouse more than dining room.

Companies call employees to the cafeteria for one of two reasons—to give them very good news or, more often, very bad news. Furey gave us the bad news. He put up a slide before us. It showed graphically—and all too dramatically —the descent our market share had suffered. It was simple, he said. If we didn't change the direction of that one trend, we had no future within IBM, none.

But after filling us with a sense of desperation, Furey did something else. He showed us the mark of a leader. He gave us hope. He went on to assure us our decline could not only be halted but reversed. And he began to lay before us his vision. Not only were we going to build Silverlake and in half the time, but, he promised us, in five years, we were going to be the number one force in the global market for mid-range computers. And we were going to make IBM Rochester the center for innovation and corporate renewal for the entire company.

He sounded so confident, and we wanted to believe. But

if Furey knew we could pull this off, he knew something else we didn't fully appreciate either—just how hard it would be. First, Furey had saddled himself with a massive undertaking. To transform his vision into a reality, he had to make good on "Drucker's dictum." Management consulting guru Peter Drucker has postulated that a true leader must manage in two time frames—the present and the future. It's not enough to overcome today's problems; the true leader puts in place the plans and people to sustain success for years to come. Furey's vision called for him to manage in *three* time frames. Ongoing plans required him to finish work on upgrades to our System/36 and System/38 computers, for introduction to the market in 1986. Then he had Silverlake to build by early 1988. And, beyond that, he had to make good on his promise to us—to turn IBM Rochester into a gemstone of IBM.

Most immediately, Furey faced considerable problems inside the lab itself. Morale was way down, thanks mostly to the Fort Knox failure and the success competitors had been enjoying at our expense. Even more troubling, we really didn't have the know-how to take on Silverlake. The idea was to base Silverlake largely on the advanced architecture of the System/38. But only a third of the engineers and programmers in the lab had worked on the System/38—too few to handle a development project as massive as the one Silverlake would entail. The remaining two-thirds of our engineers and programmers didn't possess practiced skills adequate to the task.

Finally, he faced looming questions. How would we organize ourselves in a way best suited to our vision and our more concrete business objectives? And who would report to whom under Furey, and what exactly would be their mission?

Our potential market was huge. We sold computers in 120 countries. It was too large to take on in its entirety; we had to pick and choose. But where? And how?

The development effort was so big and our resources were hardly unlimited. After the money it lost on Fort Knox, IBM was hardly ready to squander more. When it came to creating Silverlake we needed to invest our resources ever so carefully, especially in product features and new technologies. But how would we possibly rank hundreds of product features and functions so we could somehow invest only where it would significantly improve our competitiveness?

To get Silverlake out in half the time it typically took, we needed to change the way we worked. We had to become much more productive. How would we re-engineer the development process to do just that?

Counting present—and potential—customers, we were looking at numbers in the hundreds of thousands, perhaps even millions. How could we tell what they really needed? The product requirements among that many customers had to be vast—and various beyond imagination. How would we know we were on the mark in giving customers what they wanted?

To make the Silverlake a success, we were going to have to bring it to the market with a bang, and then keep the thunder rolling. But how?

These were his challenges. Ours too. But in the constant upheavals that characterize life in organizations today, momentous obstacles are the rule, not the exception. So we needed more than a capable manager, someone who would not just implement and execute, someone willing and able to go beyond the cut-and-dried tasks of planning, budgeting, organizing, and controlling.

We needed a *leader*. Leaders do not move organizations ahead incrementally; they transform them. But a leader's most important task may be to create and then articulate a vision, a clear, simple, unique picture of what an enterprise can do or be. To fulfill that vision it takes the contribution of many—the vision *involves* people. Finally, a leader inspires people to do extraordinary things.

Despite all our doubts about him, Furey was proving to us he *was* a leader. He didn't let it be known back then, but Furey was also proving his mettle as a betting man. As a hobby, he owns harness-racing horses. He's been in a sulky a few times himself and, of course, he's been to the

35

track. So he knows how to assess the odds. His whole vision rested on our success in getting Silverlake to the market on time. Furey made odds on our ability to do that. He saw it as a longshot; in fact, he figured the chances at 1,000 to one. Nevertheless, Furey took the stakes. He bet on us to beat the odds.

3

PUTTING
PEOPLE
IN PLACE

This isn't working. We're completely unfocused.

— TOM FUREY, Director, IBM Rochester Development Laboratory

When Tom Furey finished spinning his dream of hope and glory for us that day in the cafeteria, the cavernous room didn't spontaneously erupt into a rally. Its walls didn't ring with cheering and chanting. There wasn't even any applause. In our polite Midwestern way, we listened attentively to Furey's call for us to create a trend-setting computer, to become the global leader of the mid-range computer market, and to resurrect ourselves into *the* market-driven model of transformation for IBM. We remained prototypically reserved. But our American Gothic stoicism actually betrayed our real reaction. When we left, went back to our offices, and started discussing it among ourselves, one thing became clear: We weren't buying any of it.

As far as we were concerned, Furey was suffering from

delusions of grandeur. Sure, we knew we were capable of knocking out Silverlake; maybe we could even get it out in half the time it normally took. But industry and company stardom? Who was he kidding? Perhaps it hadn't sunk in yet, but Furey needed to realize he was out in the boondocks now. He was talking about weaving a Saville Row suit out of corn tassels. To us, his exhortations amounted to nothing more than one of those vacuous corporate attempts at cheerleading people into working more for less.

In addition to widespread skepticism, some quarters of IBM Rochester responded with out-and-out resistance. The programmers and engineers in the System/36 shop saw Silverlake as an idea just as misguided as Fort Knox. As conceived by Pete Hansen's skunk works, the Silverlake was to be based on the same technology embodied in the more advanced—and expensive—System/38. But at the time we had a mere 20,000 System/38 customers. We had *200,000*, or ten times as many, System/36 customers. To the System/36 group's way of thinking, looking to the Silverlake as a viable replacement to the System/36 was tantamount to foisting a Mercedes on people who really needed—and could only afford—a pickup. In so doing, we'd essentially be ceding away the lion's share of our market.

Our planners went into tacit rebellion too. Flustered by Furey's constant hounding for answers to questions they never before addressed, they saw him as an interloper—a short-timer trying to change the way they'd always done things. The way they figured it, IBM Rochester was just a stopover for Furey; he'd be gone in two years—and things would get back to normal. So their attitude was, we'll just wait the SOB out.

Furey picked up on these currents. He knew enough about the Fort Knox failure to realize how crucial it was to get people to buy in to the Silverlake Project. So he launched an effort to overcome the resistance. He began hosting a series of "roundtables," usually a luncheon in his newly redecorated conference room with a dozen or so rank-

and-file lab members But Furey didn't resort to the hard sell. He didn't give pep talks and didn't lecture. He took a far more subtle approach—he listened.

Although Tom Furey isn't exactly a paragon of personal warmth—he's not one to clamp his arm around you—he quickly began establishing himself during these roundtables as a manager who wouldn't seek retribution even when put to piercing questions. Not only did he field loaded questions with equanimity, but he responded with a disarming candor. He wasn't afraid to accept blame or own up to mistakes. "You're right, we screwed up," he'd declare. When his guests saw they could open up without risking repudiation, the roundtables flourished, blooming into substantive exchanges. Furey drew people out even more with his own talent for asking probing but well-meaning questions; people seemed captivated—if not flattered—by his intellectual curiosity and his sincere interest in what they had to say.

As time went on, his rountables helped Furey do two things. First, by *answering* questions, Furey not only began to communicate his *vision* in detail to us but he started to win our hearts over to it. And, second, by *asking* as many questions as he did—simply by listening—he was able to refine it as he went on. Both helped us to overcome the problems many executives and their companies have when it comes to the "vision thing."

It's hard enough to beget a vision, harder still to articulate it, but hardest of all to get people to make it their own. For employees to embrace a vision, it has to embrace them—that is, they have to know *they* count toward achieving it, that it really can't be done without them, that it's for them, and that it's just not some manager's ambition they're being asked to fulfill. And it has to seem doable; though it may call for them to go far beyond what they ever thought capable, it still has to stand as realistically possible. By hearing us, by letting us vent, by giving us the freedom to make our own intellectual contributions toward creating and shaping a dream that was going to take *us*,

Furey sidestepped the difficulties so many other leaders have in taking a vision to a point where it becomes concrete enough and begins to make a difference.

Even at that, Furey realized that communicating and selling alone—no matter how genuinely and artfully done —could not bring our vision to fruition. And herein lies the main lesson to be learned by any organization.

Ever so rarely, a leader comes along who is charismatic enough to reshape an organization by sheer force of personality. But too often the organization that rests its future on a single figure finds itself off on a road of shifting sands. Inevitably, any leader, even those who somehow seem bigger than life, will succumb to the same vagaries of mortality as everyone else. They get tired or distracted. They fail to adapt. They get old. They die. Even the great Lee Iacocca, who raised Chrysler from the ashes, publicly came to wonder whether he had it in him to save a troubled Chrysler a second time. Sadly, he made this concession after his best and most likely successors, frustrated by Iacocca's reluctance to relinquish his crown, went off to make their marks elsewhere.

As with so many other things, time is the true test of leadership. The best leaders leave enduring legacies. They build organizations that somehow manage to carry on even after they're long gone. To do that, they *institutionalize* their values, their visions, even their accomplishments. To provide for their enterprises beyond their own inevitable departure, decline, or demise, they create organizations that exist apart from themselves. They do this by creating organizational structures, yes. But they realize that it takes more than that.

Too many managers see company reorganizations as a be-all and end-all. But all too often such reorganizations really amount to nothing more than reshuffling the deck chairs on the *Titanic*. True leaders realize that, in the end, it really comes down to people. The problems most companies face have less to do with the organizational chart and more with the names and missions that occupy the boxes in those charts. So true leaders don't just build organization structures or merely reorder them. They create infrastructures, which consist of the right organizational structures, the right missions, and the right people, with people matched to the right mission.

Six months into his tenure, Tom Furey started to do just that. He began by creating the right infrastructure, one in keeping with his vision and with Drucker's dictum—that leaders not only have to deal in today's problems but prepare for tomorrow's possibilities.

Along with all the other hurdles that stood between our vision and its fruition, Furey faced several "structural" impediments at IBM Rochester. His foremost organizational problem was that the development lab was divided into two camps: 1,800 engineers and programmers working on the System/36 in one and 600 working on the System/38 in the other.

Although they couldn't be called warring clans, neither were they brothers in arms. They were first separated by the strong and emotional ties to their respective machines—with all the resulting biases. The System/38 group saw their machine as a Corvette, a sleek, high-performance model. They looked down on the System/36 as a Chevette, an inexpensive little runabout. To the System/36 group, their machine may have been prosaic but it was prolific; it sold like corn dogs at the county fair. Those from either group couldn't be faulted for thinking as they did. Each had built machines for distinctly different markets. The System/38 group made advanced machines for sophisticated users who could afford to pay for them, usually bigger companies that put them into departments, branch offices, and other remote locations. The System/36 group made more simple, inexpensive machines for small and medium-sized businesses. It was only natural that the markets they served would shape their mindsets.

The practical reality, however, was that both groups *had* to come together to work on Silverlake. Even though the Silverlake would be based on the same inner workings—the same architecture—of the System/38, the smaller System/38 group simply wasn't big enough to take on the job of creating the Silverlake on its own. Silverlake was also a computer meant for the users of *both* machines. Since the System/36 accounted for 90 percent of our customer base, Silverlake had to embody System/36 characteristics, especially those that would make it easy to use.

This wasn't the only division at IBM Rochester. Another was manifest in its bifurcated organizational structure. IBM Rochester actually consisted of two distinct entities—the development lab and the manufacturing operation. Furey presided over the lab. But he had a co-equal, Larry Osterwise, the "site general manager" in charge of manufacturing and who, like the superintendent of an apartment building, was also responsible for all services at the site—the cafeteria, administrative services, maintenance, and so on. Both had equal standing. So no single person was in charge. Instead, they both reported to Steve Schwartz in White Plains, New York, where the IBM midrange computer group that we were part of made its headquarters.

These two peers simply had different missions and priorities, which naturally caused occasional tensions. It also made for a certain amount of organizational gamesmanship. Furey, for example, never attended the site manager's regular Monday morning meetings. Claiming he had more important matters to deal with, he sent a deputy instead.

The biggest problem about the structure, however, was that we were *part* of a business, not *the* business itself. We simply saw ourselves as functional entities—working parts of a larger whole. We designed computers. Or we engineered hardware. Or we manufactured machines. Because we didn't own the business ourselves—because we didn't see ourselves as a unit accountable to the market—we gave little thought to the strategic factors so critical to the success of a *business entity*. We paid scant attention, say, to our channels of distribution or to the independent software vendors who created so much of the applications software to be run on our machines. We didn't pay enough heed to our customers either. It was someone else's job—sales and marketing—to worry about that.

The pitfalls of our "functional" mentality became pointedly apparent when it came to planning. We did long-range planning at IBM Rochester. But we didn't do strategic planning. Strategic planning has a long-range component to it, of course, but there's more to it. Strategic planning entails understanding the environment in which a business operates. It takes into account all the forces and factors that make the players in a market behave in a certain way. It looks at options and opportunities. Our planning never gave enough credence to these other elements.

To our product planners, those responsible for translating customer needs into product specifications, you could say, "I want a computer that costs $65,000 and does these three things." They would come back and tell you, "We can give you one for $75,000 that does *four* things." But when you asked them to strategically justify the additional capability, they would shrug. If they offered a rationale, it was tantamount to saying, "We should do this because we can."

That's not good enough. There has to be a compelling market-based reason behind everything a business does. If the engineers at General Motors put their minds to it, they could probably make a station-wagon version of the Corvette. But why?

Seeing ourselves as a functional entity led to a serious form of self-underestimation. Part of the reason we met Furey's vision with so much skepticism is that we didn't think we had as much potential as Furey figured we did. We viewed ourselves strictly within the narrow confines of our separate functions. We had a certain job to do, we did it, went home at night, and came back the next day. Someone else could put it all together—and take all the glory.

Furey knew that a new structure was in order. He probably had in mind the outlines for the reorganization he wanted. But he wasn't about to come down from the mount with it. In what was another mark of his *leadership* abilities, Furey would offer guidance and broad direction, but he wanted people to reach their own conclusions. As Silverlake proceeded, many of us often found ourselves sitting in our offices agonizing over this problem or that. We'd eventually march into Furey's office with a solution only to discover he'd come to the very same answer, and far sooner.

He handled things this way because of ownership. Furey knew that if people were going to get behind Silverlake, they had to feel as though the project belonged to them. If ideas came from their heads, not his, then he could count on them to take the credit—and with credit comes possession. This was another way of involving people as active contributors to Furey's vision; it was yet another way that his vision became *our* vision.

Furey decided to let *us* reorganize the lab. He appointed a task force to come up with the new organizational structure. It was a *cross-functional team* consisting of 10 people from various parts of the lab. As he sent this task force off to its work, he made one thing absolutely clear: It was to assume nothing about who would do what within the new structure. No one, but no one, was assured of having a particular job. The structure was to be created in accordance to our vision and our mission, not to accommodate individuals.

After three months of *research*, analysis, and deliberation, the task force devised a new structure for the development lab, and it consisted of four distinct groups, each with its own very specific mission.

- The first one would handle our lineup of current products—the existing System/36 and System/38 machines. Its mission would be to deliver upgrades by 1987 that we had already promised our customers.

- The second group was to do nothing but work on Silverlake. Engineers and programmers from both the System/36 and System/38 camps would be brought together. Their mission was daunting but straightforward: Create Silverlake, a machine that would wow the market, and do it less than half the normal time.

- The third group would be charged with formulating a strategic plan. It was to lay out a blueprint not only for

Silverlake but for IBM Rochester as a whole—a map not just for the two or so years it would take to create Silverlake but for the five years or more after it came out. It was also to identify emerging technologies and assess their applicability to Silverlake and succeeding generations of the machine. All its work was to be done in accordance with the market-driven model we would embrace.

The fourth and final group was to handle the human resources function for the lab. Its main task was to help the lab people foster and enhance their skills. It would see that they had the support and resources to do their jobs. And, most of all, it was to develop new processes that could be defined, quantified, and repeated to enhance productivity and make sure we got Silverlake done on time. It would also oversee the day-to-day administration of the lab, a role that would allow Furey to concern himself more with overarching, long-term issues.

Every facet of this structure reflected our vision and mission. It took care of getting Silverlake out and making IBM Rochester an industry leader and an IBM model. It did all that by providing a focus of mission, thus fulfilling Furey's expanded version of Drucker's dictum by addressing the *three* time frames: It upgraded current products, it provided for Silverlake's creation by 1988, and it addressed our future beyond Silverlake. The structure also did something else. It satisfied three of the most important facets of any organization—focus, focus, and focus. And this organizational structure gave us focus; each group had a distinct area of concentration. For example, the group working on Silverlake wouldn't be distracted by worrying about current products. The one doing strategic plans needn't concern itself with too many administrative or personnel issues that were meant to be handled by the human resources group.

Now that he had a structure in hand, Furey was ready to staff it with key people. For his team he tapped some longtime Rochester insiders. He recruited some outsiders, including a few who had worked for him elsewhere. Most notably, however, Furey didn't hesitate to pick people who had been organizational outcasts, some of them for standing up to the folly of Fort Knox.

That Furey would call on these "black sheep" reflected another of his other most salient leadership traits. He had a certain open-mindedness about people. He was willing to accept you—with all your weaknesses—in order to get your strengths. He wasn't bothered by someone who was eccentric or difficult if they had the talent or skills that made them right for a particular job. Furey also recognized that, often, no one works harder or more loyally than the outcasts who feel compelled to prove themselves.

Once Furey picked you for a job, he gave you full rein. In fact, if you deferred to him for a decision on a matter within the sweep of your own brief, he simply refused. "That's your job," he would snap. "You decide."

Not that Furey was afraid to make a decision himself. Another one of his maxims was, "I'd rather be wrong than indecisive." He made no secret of the fact he drank of the same waters as did another Massachusetts native, General Electric Chairman Jack Welch, one of the crispest decision-makers in business. Like Welch, Furey wasn't one to waffle; he made it clear where he stood. And by articulating his vision and positions this sharply, he didn't force you to do any executive mind-reading, an endeavor that has sent many a corporate foot soldier into a stomach-churning state of equivocation. With Furey, tough decisions still had to be made, but somehow they just weren't as ulcerating to make as under other managers. He would set certain benchmarks for organizational behavior, and establish clear-cut objectives. He'd thus create the boundaries in which you could work. But within those boundaries you had the leeway to act according to your own best judgment—without any fear of being second-guessed.

To head the group that would focus on making the upgrades to the existing System/36 and System/38, Furey appointed Jeff Robertson, an IBM Rochester veteran who

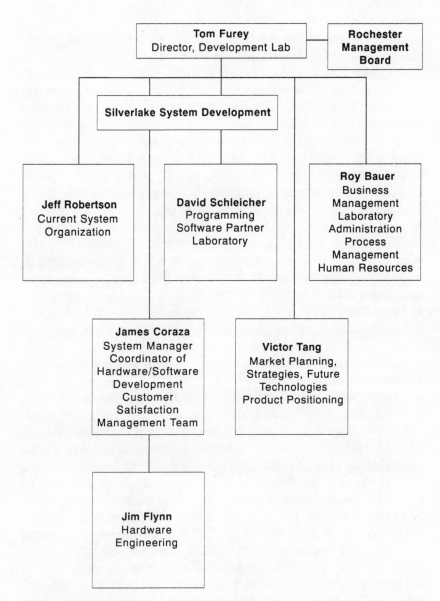

Figure 1. Organizational structure

had long been involved with the System/36 and its wide-spread success.

Furey made three key appointments to the second group, the one that would concentrate on producing the Silverlake. They were Jim Coraza, Dave Schleicher, and Jim Flynn.

Coraza, an IBM veteran who'd been the quality control executive attached to the Fort Knox project, became Silverlake's "system manager." He made sure that the two distinct development tasks involved in Silverlake—the software and hardware—meshed into a smooth-working computer "system." Coraza's background made him a keen choice. He had previous experiences with projects of a grand scale, and Silverlake was nothing if not grand. His quality control background also meant that he brought an interdisciplinary mentality to the job. Quality in any product is the sum of all its aspects—design, engineering, manufacturing, marketing, and sales. As a quality manager, Coraza was accustomed to dealing with various and disparate functions. If Silverlake was going to be a success, everything would have to come together just so. Coraza's job was to see that it did.

Coraza's role as grand coordinator was extremely crucial. Because so many of our existing customers were overseas, the Silverlake, from its inception, was meant to be a *global* product. In the past, we'd always made our computers available for shipment in the United States first and then to Europe and elsewhere six months or more later. But Furey intended to give the Silverlake a worldwide launch, seeing that it would simultaneously be available to customers in the 120 countries where we did business. Consequently, Silverlake would be one of IBM's most complex undertakings. It would be manufactured on three continents —with components supplied by 37 different IBM locations throughout the world. Silverlake's software not only had to be created quickly, it also needed to be translated into 27 different languages and dialects. Field engineers and sales representatives would have to be trained all over the globe.

It was mind-boggling. But one of the most notable traits about Coraza was that he just didn't boggle—there was no more imperturbable character. If Coraza was angry or anxious, you never knew it from his demeanor. And if something as complicated as the Silverlake project was going to come off, a cool head, like Coraza's, had to prevail.

Schleicher was tapped to head the 1,200 programmers who would crank out Silverlake's software. He grew up on a farm in southeastern Minnesota and had come to work at IBM Rochester in 1971 as a programmer. He rose through the ranks to manage the entire programming side of the lab, a job he'd held about five years before Furey's arrival. There was very little in software development, at any level, that he did not have a strong expertise in.

Software programming is a bit like writing a novel. It's a creative process; certainly it's at least as much art as science. But artistic types can be notoriously undisciplined, given to awaiting the muse to move them. One of Schleicher's most notable achievements as director of software development was to institute certain tools and measures that brought discipline to writing software code, one that would eventually see the Silverlake Project through some of its toughest moments. It was also this discipline that made IBM Rochester the most productive software development center in IBM. From the beginning we estimated that the Silverlake would require some 7 million lines of software code, three times more than any of our machines. And if we wanted to churn out that much code in half the time, we needed discipline more than anything else.

If a temperamental opposite to Coraza existed, it was Jim Flynn, a chain-smoking, coffee-chugging engineer. Flynn was picked to oversee the creation of Silverlake's hardware. His job was to engineer the processors of varying power for each of the six different models of the Silverlake we planned to offer at system prices of between $15,000 and $1 million. High-strung and driven, Flynn wasn't afraid to make waves if it involved something important. It was nothing for him to pepper the E-mail system with memos all the way up IBM's executive chain of command if that's what was needed to drive home a point.

49

Flynn cared a lot about the Silverlake Project and saw it as the way to rehabilitation. He'd been among those who openly opposed Fort Knox and had gotten into hot water. As a result, he took on his Silverlake assignment with a zeal of one obsessed with settling an old score.

To head the third group, the one with the mission to create the strategy for the Silverlake Project and beyond, Furey reached to an association from his past. He recruited Vic Tang. The son of an ambassador, Tang had lived among several different cultures and spoke four languages. A mathematician and engineer by education, he had a track record as an IBM software and hardware development manager and spent time out in the field, among customers, in systems engineering. From the field he was picked for a series of headquarters assignments. There, finding himself challenged by broad business issues, he decided to concentrate on strategic planning. To add substance to aspiration, Tang earned an advanced degree in business.

He originally hooked up with Furey at IBM's Kingston, New York, development lab, where, as a strategic planning manager, he helped conceive the niche strategy that made a go of the large computer screen venture Furey had managed. Tang, who was at once a methodical and restless man, brought a conceptual bent to his job. And because of his multi-functional experience, he brought an integrative perspective as well. He was equally comfortable with marketing, technology, and finance. And perhaps because he'd been exposed to so many places and cultures, he had a way of thinking that was global. He was also known, when the chips were down, as a manager who would deliver the goods.

At first, Tang demurred at Furey's offer to move to Minnesota; he and his family hardly relished the thought of leaving the metropolitan diversity of New York. But, because the Mayo Clinic and IBM draw expertise from around the world, Rochester happens to have an active international community. It even publishes its own Chinese language newsletter, and Furey saw to it that Tang and his family started getting it at home in White Plains. The gambit worked, and within weeks after turning Furey down, they were packing for life on the prairie.

To head the fourth group, the one to oversee the human resources and day-to-day operations of the lab, Furey turned to another longtime IBM Rochester employee, Roy Bauer. Bauer was a mechanical engineer by education. He joined IBM Rochester in 1967 and, for all but a two-year stint in a corporate staff job as manager of manufacturing engineering out East, he remained true to his roots and committed himself to staying in Minnesota. Bauer moved up to eventually lead the hard disk manufacturing business at Rochester, an "intrapraneurial" enterprise that made drives not only for IBM computers but for sale in the open market (something IBM had never done before). In his spare time, he wrote personal computer programs, many for small businesses, which offered him a unique perspective —one that helped him see things from the user's point of view.

A year before Furey came along, Bauer was promoted into a job that put him in charge of IBM Rochester's 1,000-person site operations organization, supervising everything from the information-processing systems, other administrative services, and security to maintenance—no small challenge for a place with as much square footage as 75 football fields, eight miles of corridors, and one of the largest computer centers in IBM.

Over the years, Bauer had proven himself a good general manager. But, more than anything, he was known as a consummate "people" person. In IBM's annual employee surveys, Bauer rated higher than almost anyone else on measures of employee approval and interpersonal skills. In fact, when Furey and Bauer first met—at a get-acquainted gathering Furey held with all key managers—they got to perusing those survey results. Furey saw Bauer's ratings and asked, "Why don't you come over and work some of that magic on the lab?" With morale down, Furey certainly needed a wizard. Bauer declined. But when Furey made a second pass, Bauer accepted. He'd always been intrigued by the lab, and this would give him the chance finally to be part of something involving the earmarks of a complete business. Bauer took charge of nurturing the skill base and processes of the lab. And when Furey was absent, Bauer, as overseer of the daily doings, ran the group by proxy.

After reorganizing and restaffing, other managers probably would have viewed their work as done. Not Furey. He knew it would take an enormous amount of coordination to get the Silverlake out on time. Everyone—in the lab and outside—at IBM Rochester had to be on the same wavelength; consensus was absolutely crucial. Furey also needed some way to get his arms around the parts of IBM Rochester—manufacturing, for example—over which he asserted no direct control.

He addressed the issues of communication, consensus, and control by borrowing an organizational idea from the corporation's upper councils, a group called the Corporate Management Board. It consists of the chairman, executive vice presidents, and the heads of all major IBM business units. Board members meet frequently to review major issues and create a forum in which major decisions can be discussed, if not reached.

Furey decided to create an analogue of the Corporate Management Board at IBM Rochester. He called it, unsurprisingly enough, the Rochester Management Board, or the RMB for short. It consisted of the 18 top decision-makers at IBM Rochester—Furey, along with Coraza, Schleicher, Flynn, Tang, Bauer, and a few of their chief lieutenants, as well as Site General Manager Larry Osterwise and the heads of manufacturing, finance, sales, and marketing. The RMB met every other Thursday, from 8 a.m. to noon. Its members were free to bring up or take on any issue and debate was encouraged. Just by getting all those people in one room on a regular basis, the RMB also became a conduit for keeping everyone at IBM Rochester fully apprised of all pertinent issues involving the Silverlake.

Not long after its creation, the RMB faced its first test. IBM Europe, which had great success in selling the System/36, came to us with a special request: They wanted us to build an extra-small version of the System/36, one priced at about \$11,000 or \$5,000 below the smallest existing System/36 model. Europe wanted the new machine for two reasons. First, they saw a need for it in businesses too big to depend on a personal computer and too small to afford a full-blown System/36. Second, they regarded it as a defensive move—a way to keep as many customers as possible in the fold until we could hit the market with the Silverlake.

The request became the focus of a huge controversy—the development lab, finance, and even U.S. marketing fervently opposed it. They argued that the effort would consume precious resources at a time when we needed to marshal everything toward the Silverlake. Besides, they said, the new machine would steal potential customers away from the smaller Silverlake models planned. Furey let everyone have their say. In fact, his practice was to point to each member of the RMB gathered around the long table in his conference room and ask, "What's your position on this?"

Views remained evenly split. We debated, sometimes heatedly, for weeks. Furey, who maintained a rather Solomonic presence, wasn't satisfied with the arguments on either side. So he ordered Tang to make a full-blown strategic study of the proposal. After three months of *research and modeling*, Tang and his team recommended that we produce the little machine and presented a detailed analysis in support of this position. With the analysis before them and satisfied that they'd been able to vent their views, opponents quickly relented. Everyone signed on. The result: We got the new computer out in a mere 12 months. In the year after that, we racked up sales of the small computer to the tune of 50,000 units. Our decision to build it paid off, in spades.

While the RMB helped us cope with our own organizational dynamics, we faced what may have been an even more daunting challenge in dealing with the prodigious corporate hierarchy beyond our walls. To get the Silverlake out, we knew we "had to make the elephant tap dance." It wouldn't be easy, and not only because the beast was so big. Sheer distance played a role too. We were 1,500 miles away from our group's White Plains headquarters and all those miles put us at a disadvantage. Other key IBM operational sites are only an hour's drive from the nerve centers of White Plains and Armonk. If one of our counterparts had a vested interest in some matter being considered by the upper councils, they could just zip over and represent themselves. Their proximity also meant they could more readily stay atop the dynamics of headquarters personalities and politics that often affect the fates of those out in the field.

We had no such luxury. We couldn't schmooze on a routine basis with the powers-that-be. If something came up affecting our interests, we couldn't be there to represent ourselves at the drop of a hat. Distance made it infinitely more difficult to use the grappling hook of personal influence that would make the elephant step, let alone do a jig.

To overcome these disadvantages, Furey made an innovative and unusual organizational move. He did for IBM Rochester what corporations routinely do when dealing with government capitols—he employed what was, in effect, a lobbyist. But instead of representing us before some distant legislature, Furey's lobbyist was to oversee our interests within the higher circles of IBM. In doing this, Furey did not resort to pretense. IBM routinely sends people on temporary assignment to sites all around the world. At IBM Rochester, people were always going off to Armonk, Japan, or other far-flung parts of the company. Furey just put someone on "assignment" in White Plains.

Our emissary was Jack Bell, a friend and former colleague of Furey's from his days in White Plains. If there was ever a person to deal with IBM's bureaucracy for us, Bell was perfect. A big man, and a native New Yorker, Bell struck you with his Queens-bred, street-savvy presence, which gave him a certain charm. But instead of the streets, Bell's smarts were for the inner workings of IBM. A career spent around and in the upper echelons of the company as a sales and marketing executive equipped him with incredible connections. He knew everyone who was anyone at IBM —on a first-name basis. He could work the organization like an old ward heeler.

From his post in White Plains, Bell would act on key business decisions without our being there. More important, he became an invaluable source of intelligence. If IBM had cranked out an important marketing study, Bell would make certain we got a copy. More than once, we used such studies to defend a strategic decision we made. Bell also sat in on Schwartz's staff meetings and kept us apprised of significant developments. He would even report to Furey on the subtle dynamics of these meetings—to the extent that he would report the reactions, right down to body language, that people had to certain matters.

Bell's presence was not covert. Schwartz knew about the arrangement, and he approved—probably because it served Schwartz as well. After all, Schwartz probably saw Bell as a way to keep tabs on us to the same extent that Bell helped us keep tabs on the doings in White Plains.

During these early phases of the Silverlake project, Furey created one other organizational structure. At the time, many of us thought him off the wall because what he did was so premature. Furey established a *cross-functional* customer satisfaction team. He did this because we had real trouble dealing with customers when something went wrong—no one at IBM Rochester "owned" the customer's problem. If the field engineers or sales representatives couldn't resolve a problem, they referred it to sales and marketing higher-ups in Rochester. If sales and marketing couldn't fix it, they kicked the complaint to manufacturing. If manufacturing didn't know what went awry, they threw it over to programming, and so on. The complaint just bounced around, until the customer blew up. Only then were we galvanized to get something done—and by then it was usually too late to rescue our relationship with the customer.

Furey intended to rectify this situation through the customer satisfaction group. It consisted of eight people from marketing, planning, manufacturing, engineering, and service. He put another of those Rochester bulldogs in charge: Jim Harens, the type of person who simply wouldn't be called off a problem once it was in his jaws. If something came up, it went to Harens' group. In the team Furey established accountability. He could hold them accountable and they, by extension, could hold us accountable as well. In meetings of the RMB—where the customer satisfaction team gave regular reports—Furey could turn to Harens and say, "Okay, how exactly are you going to deal with this?" The customer satisfaction team did something else too. By tracing problems back to their root cause, we could deal with them at their source, where we could fix them once and for all.

Since Silverlake was still on the drawing boards, the customer satisfaction group was ostensibly formed to deal with problems involving the System/36 and System/38. Yet Furey had the group reporting to Coraza, with overall system responsibility for the Silverlake. Furey had his reasons, of course. He wanted to raise the whole notion of customer satisfaction to a much higher profile in our minds by connecting it to the project that would become the centerpiece of our lives and survival. Right from the beginning of our efforts, Furey wanted to instill in us the customer satisfaction ethic. After all, customer satisfaction is *the* hallmark of a *market-driven* enterprise. Customers *are* the market.

By the fall of 1986, we had the framework in place to fulfill his vision. And even if the fates had somehow interceded to take Furey away from us, we were in a position to carry on. His vision had become *our* vision, and we had an organization and people in place to bring it to reality.

If there's an object lesson for others in what we did it's that reorganizing alone isn't enough. Too many managers think they can solve all their problems by remapping the organization charts. Not so; much more is needed. Of course, an element of architecture is involved. Ad hoc groups, like our own Rochester Management Board, can go a long way toward fostering communication and cooperation. The structure of an enterprise should reflect its vision and, certainly, its business objectives in a focused way. The real key, however, is picking the right people and making sure a match exists between those people—their skills, experience, and strengths—and a *well-defined mission*. Once those people are in the right place and given an appropriate mission, they must be allowed their rein, trusted to do what needs to be done. This is the most certain way leaders can institutionalize their legacies.

Within months after the Silverlake Project was underway we had the structures and people in place to bring our new machine to life—*and* to fulfill our vision of transforming IBM Rochester into a model for all of IBM. Dreams are nice. But now we had to get down to the nitty-gritty work involved in making dreams come true. And we had to start with basics. When we did, we found out we couldn't adequately answer some very fundamental questions: Who bought our machines and why. Without those answers, the Silverlake Project, along with all our dreams, would almost certainly remain that—a dream.

4

GETTING TO KNOW OUR CUSTOMERS

Who are our customers?

— MAGGIE MCNALLY, Manager of Market Research, IBM Rochester

As the Silverlake Project revved up, we began asking ourselves a few questions. Actually, we asked two, both very basic. But they were also profound. The reason: Nearly everything about our new machine rested on how we answered those two questions.

Although we had a basic design, the answers would determine many of the choices we still had to make from among a 2,000-item laundry list of possible product characteristics, including how fast the machine would operate, how much memory it would have, what programming languages it would comprehend, and what software programs it would run. They also would go to the heart of every decision about our machine beyond the design phase. They were the key to setting its price tag, launching it into the marketplace, even creating advertisements for it.

In short, the entire strategy for our machine—our whole

future in the mid-range market—hinged on the answers to two questions:

Who are our customers?

What do they want?

Incredible as it may sound, no one at IBM Rochester had an adequate answer. Our inability didn't make us an exception, though. We were like so many other enterprises that fail to even *ask* themselves these fundamental questions. Without posing them, without answering them, an enterprise can't possibly know its markets. And if it doesn't know its markets, it can't possibly stay abreast of customer needs and wants. And if it doesn't stay in touch with what its customers need and want—especially in a world where needs and wants can change in a blink—it faces the gravest danger of all, that of misjudging or missing a market.

Worse, if an enterprise doesn't know its markets, it doesn't know itself, and can't possibly know what it's supposed to do or be. In other words, it can't possibly say what business it's in, not precisely and not concretely. And if it doesn't know what business it's in beyond insipid generalities, it's probably doomed to make errant sidetrips into ventures for which it has neither resources, experience, skills, and whatever else it takes to effectively compete.

As we began asking those two questions at IBM Rochester, we got responses typified by those from a meeting in August 1986, when Vic Tang first put them to his strategic planning group—the very people who would be mapping the overall plan for getting our machine off the drawing board and into the marketplace. Who are our customers? Someone raised a hand. "Boeing is a customer. I was out there to visit last week." But that answer was far too anecdotal; we needed something much more encompassing. "Our customers are buyers of mid-range computers," someone else offered. "They're users of software packages for business," another planner chimed in. But those were too broad, so generalized and squishy as to be useless.

Our inability to come up with a good reply actually said

59

a lot—it spoke volumes about our understanding of our market. Yes, we could produce customer lists. But no one could answer in a *conceptual* way that was at the same time concrete enough to serve as the basis for executing a substantive business decision, let alone an entire strategy. We'd never even tried to answer in a methodical way through *research and modeling*. What we knew about our customers, we got anecdotally, either from contacts we'd had ourselves or from what our sales representatives in the field told us.

And if we didn't know who our customers were, it only followed that we certainly didn't know what they needed. We *thought* we knew. At IBM Rochester, we harbored an arrogantly paternalistic regard for our customers. Like an overbearing parent who presumes to know what's right for their adult children, we assumed that our experience and expertise allowed us to know what was best for our customers. In an earlier era, that might be true. When computers were still a novelty, we no doubt knew more than anybody about using the machines we invented and made.

But by 1986, the market had changed. Unfortunately, our mentality hadn't. As computers became ubiquitous and their use suffused every aspect of life, customers became more and more sophisticated. They knew computers all right. And they knew their own businesses better than we ever could. Yet we persisted in presuming we knew what they needed without really trying to find out. And with the growing number of competitors coming into the mid-range market, we no longer had the luxury of being able to impose our presumptions. If we weren't serving customers' needs, they could choose others who could.

Of course, we weren't stone deaf to customer needs. But when we did listen, we listened to the wrong ones. Small and medium-sized businesses used our mid-range computers. But when it came to putting capability into our machines, these weren't the customers who carried the most weight. Instead, we gave more credence to the wishes of big customers, mostly Fortune 500 companies. This represented a characteristic IBM bias—one that emerged from our peculiar "mainframe mentality." IBM rose to the reaches of corporate size and prestige by making and selling mainframes, which are large, powerful, and expensive computers—"big iron" in the lingo of the industry. Big iron has always accounted for the lion's share of IBM's overall revenues. Everyone who's anyone within IBM usually came from that side of the business; if you wanted to ascend the ranks, you had to have mainframe experience among your credits.

Traditionally, big customers buy big iron. And the people directly responsible for making those buying decisions for big customers are the information-processing executives who keep the keys to the "glass house," the euphemism used in industry circles for the special air-conditioned rooms in which mainframes are usually contained. Companies also frequently put their mainframes in glass-enclosed rooms so they could show them off. IBM really catered to the glass-house executives. And who could blame it? That's where the money was.

IBM's focus was fine during the days when the glass house controlled all computing resources as a single fiefdom even in the most far-flung corporations. If we wanted to sell mid-sized computers for a corporation's satellite locations, the purchase order still had to be okayed from the glass house. But as computer size and price shrank, and as information-processing capability was distributed to the corporation's farthest reaches, people outside headquarters started making computer purchasing decisions themselves. The glass house began losing control; the people there weren't calling all the shots anymore, especially when it involved buying mid-sized machines.

This change went largely overlooked by us as we adhered to our old bias. When our salespeople told us that customer so-and-so needed this capability or that, we listened, never mind that they were voicing the interests of a giant customer who could make or break their quotas for the year. Or when top executives started dabbling in functionality decisions based on what they'd been hearing from customers, you could guess it was because they'd just had lunch with one of our big-blue chip corporate users.

The bottom line is that we knew about very large customers. But what else we thought we knew about other customers we frequently divined on the basis of incomplete information and by intuition. We don't want to downplay the importance of gut feelings in business. But we erred by relying too much on instinct and not enough on a thorough, hardnosed look at our market.

And the market for Silverlake begged for analysis, if only for a single overarching reality: It was so huge. The market for mid-sized computers spans a yawning price range. By conventional definition, it includes machines priced anywhere between $15,000 and $1 million. In aggregate terms, we estimated the overall market for mid-range systems at over $200 billion over the strategic period. Our market encompassed the world—more than 60 percent of Silverlake's predecessor machines were sold overseas. We literally had customers on every continent. Our market wasn't only big, it was diverse. We had customers in practically every line of business imaginable—insurance, manufacturing, distribution, transportation, shipping, and government, to name just a few. They ranged in size from just a few to thousands.

Another factor contributed to our murky market understanding, and it shows how certain developments can affect a company to its core. In January 1969, the U.S. Department of Justice filed an anti-trust suit against IBM, drawing the company into an extraordinarily long and complex legal battle that lasted until its withdrawal in 1982. Justice accused IBM of monopolizing the market for mid-range commercial computers. But as its main defense, IBM contended that the charges described a much too narrow unrealistic market. IBM argued that if you defined the market to include not just mid-range commercial computers, but everything else that went into the business —high-end, low-end, scientific computers, printers, disk drives, software, . . . —then IBM wasn't dominant at all.

What did this have to do with our ability to know our market? Since the case hinged on how you defined the market, everyone in the company became paranoid about describing markets in anything but the broadest possible terms, particularly in confidential memos and other intra-company communications. IBM feared it would provide Justice with a smoking gun for market definition. We even went so far as to avoid using the word "market." Instead, we used "customers" when we really wanted to say "market." In a testament to the power of language, using this euphemism led to a subtle, intuitive leap in our thinking. By substituting "customers" for "markets," we started equating the entire market with our base of *existing* customers. We gave no mind to *potential* customers. We subliminally just wrote off a portion of the business by not even trying to get it.

By 1985, we had paid a dear price by competing in such a big and indistinct market without dissecting it. Not knowing our customers and what they really wanted came back to haunt us—and with a vengeance.

We started missing the mark with our machines. Take the System/38. Although it attracted an intensely loyal group of users, it never really caught on. Why? Its advanced features didn't capture the fancy of the marketplace—we never made it clear how that technology could satisfy the real needs of our customers. This particular failing was symptomatic of another wrongheaded aspect of our institutional mentality. We had become a "product-driven" enterprise.

We became obsessed with the machines themselves, their design and engineering—not with how our customers would use them. We cared more about our own sensibilities as computer purists. We were like Formula One racers trying to create a family car. We kept coming up with something that still looked like a hot rod. This proclivity became most apparent when we'd talk among ourselves about a new machine. We'd spend 90 percent of the time discussing technological specifications, or what was inside the box. What was lost on us is that customers don't usually care about a machine's innards. It could be filled with mush, just as long as it helps them run their business efficiently. Instead, we kept giving customers these marvels of modern engineering—marvels in search of a problem to solve.

Compatibility was also becoming a bigger concern to customers. When they bought a new machine with more power and capacity, they didn't want to "junk" all the software they'd paid so much to create or buy. They wanted to be able to "migrate" those applications to the new machine. But did we hear them? Hardly. As a successor to the IBM 1130, one of the company's earlier mid-range computers, IBM produced the IBM System 7. But applications on the 1130 could not be used directly on the System 7. Customers complained. What did we do? As a successor to System 7, we created the IBM Series 1, a mid-range computer offered to the market by the early 1980s. Did System 7 software work on the Series 1? Of course not.

But the most telling statement of our wrongheadedness was the failure of Fort Knox. By trying to create a single replacement machine for customers moving up from our System/36, System/38, and three other mid-range computers made by other parts of IBM, we wanted Fort Knox to be "all things to all people". When a market is small enough you can do that, but not in one as massive as that for mid-range computers. If you do, you wind up with an average product that satisfies almost no one. By trying to build a machine for such a diffused market, Fort Knox turned out to be infeasible and we lost millions of dollars. Worse, we missed a product cycle, which meant we lost time and ground to the competition.

With so much riding on Silverlake, we couldn't afford to make the same mistakes. We had to dissect the market to know who our customers were, who they could be, and what they really wanted. We needed to give Silverlake more focus so it wouldn't become a mundane machine meant to be used by everyone and, therefore, no one.

We needed a strategy for Silverlake. And the foundation for that strategy—a plan encompassing design, production, sales, and marketing—had to include an excruciatingly analytical look at our markets, our customers, and their needs. To do that, Vic Tang initiated an effort based on something taught in every graduate business school marketing class. He decided to *segment* our market into its component parts. Then he was going to have us *target* certain segments. We could then *position* Silverlake in those markets so that it would be clearly distinguished from its competition.

What you learn in every marketing class is that no market is homogeneous and customer needs vary widely. But markets can be broken down into components that are quite nearly homogeneous. You can segment a market in several ways—by geography, size, industry, age group, needs, and so forth. Ultimately, the best segmentation is to break a market down to its most basic unit of absorption. Once you've got a market segmented, you can pick and choose which to target. You can target markets on the basis of any number of criteria—whether they'll meet certain revenue or profit goals or whether you can reach them via certain channels of sales and distribution.

Once you've found segments to focus on, the final step is to differentiate your product from the competition. This involves positioning, probably *the* most important step in becoming a market-driven company. Positioning is the reason customers buy your product. Good positioning distinguishes a product from the competition based on what the customer *thinks* is important. Bufferin is a common product that has been masterfully positioned by its makers. Its positioning is captured in a simple line: A painkiller that's gentle to your stomach. That line articulates Bufferin's key benefit to the consumer—it relieves pain—and goes on to differentiate itself from its competition, namely aspirin, which can irritate your stomach.

All this sounds straightforward enough. But it would take Tang and his team some doing to embody these concepts in our strategy. The effort took 18 months of taxing work that eventually involved as many as 25 people. Along the way, we faced enormous obstacles. One of the first was getting our strategic planning group simply to comprehend what we wanted to do. At the outset, they had trouble.

When we used terms typical to the strategic planning process—terms such as "market infrastructure"—they didn't know what we meant. This had nothing to do with their IQs; it actually reflected an institutional shortcoming.

Until Tang arrived, IBM Rochester didn't do long-term, conceptual strategic planning. Instead, any planning tended to be short term and tactical. What's the difference? Let's put it this way: In the 1991 Gulf War, coalition military commanders had a war *strategy*—to isolate, starve, and weaken the Iraqi army and oust it from Kuwait. The *tactics* at their disposal included air bombardment, cruise missile attacks, amphibious landings and a flanking ground attack. At IBM Rochester, our bent toward tactical maneuvering manifested itself in the staff positions that the vast majority of our planning people formally occupied. They were either product planners or business planners.

To product planners belonged the task of taking concrete customer needs and translating them into product features. If they had worked at Ford, say, they're the people who would have been told, "We want a medium-priced car of Japanese quality and German engineering meant for a middle-class family." Given those parameters, they would have come up with the specifications for a car that looked a lot like a Taurus. But it was beyond them to question the need for a Taurus in the first place. By the time the Silverlake Project came along, we needed people who would say, "Well, the real growth market isn't for a family car but for something more sporty for yuppies without any children."

Our product planners usually came from sales. Why? Because they were closest to the customer, which was true enough. But people in sales are brought up in a side of the business that emphasizes the tactical, not the strategic. Their horizon tends to stretch out only to this year's quota or commission—their whole mentality gets shaped by doing only what it takes to get that far to succeed.

Our business planners tended toward a tactical orientation, as well. Business planners are financial types. Their main job was to track and predict the progress we were making toward quarterly or annual financial goals. Their longer forecasts were straightline extrapolations based on current circumstances—a kind of "ruler planning" that neglected to consider very many market variables. For the most part, if we announced a product in January, these are the folks who would have said, "We expect to sell 30,000 by December, but most of those orders won't come in until the third and fourth quarters so that's how the revenues will flow."

Fortunately, we were learning quickly. In fact, our first breakthrough toward segmenting the market came from one of our managers. He was Bob Cooper, a former IBM salesman with a flair for insightful and useful market analysis. He was a hulking former college football player with a buoyant sense of humor. People called Cooper the "Monster of the Mid-Range," a takeoff on the "Monsters of the Midway" nickname given to the Chicago Bears because of his tenacity in tackling tough business problems.

Cooper's breakthrough came when he began looking into a study done by a market research group at headquarters. This study, one of dozens that come out of the various nooks at IBM each year, was based on a certain premise—to quantify and understand the demand for computers you have to look at the number of *locations* where they are used and what they are used for. This little bit of insight sent light bulbs snapping on over our collective heads. Because we had become so product driven up to then, we'd considered the source of demand—our customers—not as the places where our computers were actually used but as the entity whose name was on the checks issued to buy the machines. We had conditioned ourselves to view our customers only as the legally constituted unit in which they were embodied—the corporation, the company, the partnership, or the governmental agency. We thought of them principally as *enterprises*.

They were. The U.S. Department of Agriculture was a customer. But so were the 2,400 locations—nearly every county in the country—into which it had installed one of our System/36 machines to administer its mammoth farm subsidies program. This distinction became particularly important with locations—branch offices, satellite plants —that often made their own buying decisions, separate from those at the enterprise's headquarters.

By thinking of our customers in their form as enterprises only, we had imposed an artificial limitation on ourselves. We were discounting a whole class of customers—the *establishments* or locations where our computers were used. It was a blind spot that the competition really took advantage of. Our market share slide had less to do with losing customers than our failing to attract new ones in a growing segment. When we realized this, we had a major new conceptual answer to the question, Who are our customers? They were enterprises *and* establishments. Both served as the ultimate unit of absorption for our computers. This way of classifying our customers could be applied to our market anywhere on the globe.

Somewhere in the neighborhood of 50 million enterprises in the world are present and potential computer users. There are *65 million* establishments. So our dissecting obviously had to go further. We knew we had customers of varying size, and size was a distinction that cut across international boundaries as well. We also sensed a strong correlation between the size of a customer and the particular way a computer got used. So we decided that we would slice the market up by establishment and enterprise size —small, medium, and large. This way, we would know where and how the establishments were distributed; for example, how many small establishments are part of a medium or large enterprise. Then, we figured we could break down the market along another parameter—by industry and then by sub-industry. When got this far, you could finally determine how customers of a certain location size, industry, and sub-industry were actually *using* the computer. In other words, we could pinpoint what a customer needed and wanted.

Cooper took this game plan and applied it to a single U.S. industry—health care. Using data obtained from the

U.S. Bureau of Labor Statistics, Cooper broke the industry down by location size, based on employment. Examples included hospitals, hospital departments, pharmacies, clinics, doctor's offices, and medical laboratories of various sorts. He also found an IBM analysis that showed what computers each of these locations used and their propensity to buy again. Using this IBM "win-loss" study, he was able to tell why users in health care bought certain computers and not others.

Cooper's dogged work led to some major discoveries. First, since we knew the health-care industry by location size and propensity to buy, we could come up with numbers to show approximately how many machines were likely to be bought. Second, and even more important, Cooper's dissection told us that the machine itself—the hardware—was only part of the purchase decision. It was by no means even the primary one. Factors such as software and service played pivotal roles. If anything, software programs, the applications users depended on for billing, admissions, patient records, and so on, topped the list of reasons why customers bought computers. This brought us closer to a new and pivotal understanding about our business: Customers didn't really buy machines, they bought *solutions* to satisfy certain business needs. We had taken the first step from being a product-driven company to being a market-driven one.

We knew we had set out on the right path during the spring of 1987. George Conrades had just been named head of the IBM business unit that IBM Rochester belonged to. (We reported to Schwartz in White Plains and Schwartz reported to Conrades.) As is typical for a new executive to a key post, Conrades began a round of visits to the various sites under his jurisdiction to learn, firsthand, the lay of the land. When he arrived in Rochester, we rolled out the red carpet. After all, Conrades occupied a place just a single rung below the very top of IBM. We mustered our 12 top people for an all-day briefing to acquaint Conrades with the doings underway at IBM Rochester.

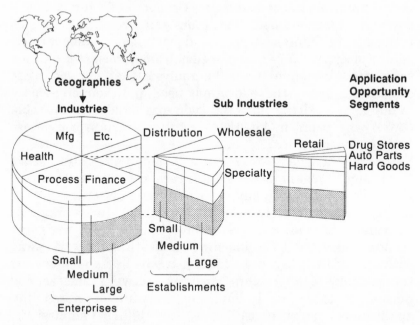

Figure 2. Market analysis and segmentation

Early on in this meeting, Conrades made it clear he was looking for answers to a few basic questions: Who are our customers? And what do they want? He also expressed a consternation that he hadn't gotten satisfactory answers during some of his other site visits. Not long after he made that statement we hit him with the findings of our health-care industry segmentation analysis. As we laid it out for him, he kept nodding. Finally, we told him this represented what would be the overall basis for strategic planning for Silverlake and IBM Rochester as a whole. He said, "You certainly have the underpinnings." Those words may not seem like much; he didn't stand up, slap any of us on the back, and begin to sing high praises for our analytical brilliance. But in the button-down world of IBM, those words amounted to a ringing endorsement.

Carrying on, however, confronted us with a massive challenge. We had segmented just one industry in one geography, the U.S. But we considered ourselves a global player. We wanted to segment the markets for the United States, all of North and South America, the major nations of Europe, and for Asia, including Japan. We wanted a breakdown of enterprises and establishments in all those places. We wanted them all classified by three sizes—small, medium, and large. Then we wanted a breakdown by industry and then, by sub-industry. We also wanted to establish the most important software applications used by customers. Finally, we wanted to forecast demand five years out. The permutations resulting from the combination of all these parameters would number in the millions.

To manage this herculean task, we turned to Emilio Collar, a man not easily intimidated. As a young Cuban revolutionary, he helped overthrow the corrupt pre-Castro dictatorship. But when Castro's Cuba proved to be no less totalitarian, Collar turned against the new regime and became a leader of an underground student movement. Forced to flee for his life, he eventually wound up in the United States. When he arrived in America, Collar knew no English. He learned it on his own, got an economics degree, and wound up with a job at IBM. He rose through the ranks of finance, and in the early 1980s, was serving as chief financial officer for IBM Rochester's disk drive business. He was tapped for the segmentation job because, along with his financial acumen, he had shown a natural propensity to think strategically.

Collar began creating the *models*, methods, and processes for analyzing the data and building it into a huge database, one that never before existed for such information. Collar and a team of 25 others broke entire industries down to their smallest available denominator, such as the type of businesses that made up an industry, the size of those businesses, the number of enterprises and establishments, even the kinds of jobs they encompassed. They got IBM geographic units in Europe and Japan to grind out the same analysis. They also created a computer model that could impute and forecast demand by enterprise and establishment size and by industry, based on such factors as the

71

propensity to automate, even the level of computer literacy among employees. When this information was linked with industry growth, employment growth, and capital spending trends, the model began to paint a picture for us—one that would permit us to start narrowing down literally thousands of potential markets to only the most promising ones. And once we began to do that, we could look into ways of satisfying customer needs in those specific markets.

Indeed, to understand the needs of customers as thoroughly as we could, we formed *cross-functional teams*, each consisting of people from engineering, programming, planning, manufacturing, and marketing. We assigned a single industry to each team. The team owned the mission of finding out everything it could about the industry that it was assigned to. Team members talked to consultants and analysts familiar with each of those industries and visited customers as well.

When all this information and analysis starting coming together, some startling discoveries resulted. Demand for mid-range computers like Silverlake did not exist where we at IBM Rochester always thought it did. We found out that large customers—those with 5,000 or more employees at a single location—accounted for a minuscule percentage of total demand for mid-range systems. In the United States, large customers, defined in this way, numbered only 15,000. Yet this was the segment we gave our most devoted attention to. In reality, small to medium-sized establishments and enterprises constituted the lion's share of demand. More than 85 percent of demand came from establishments of less than 5,000 employees—and they represented the growth in the mid-range market. We found, for example, that small and medium-sized business had been expanding at two to three times the rate of Fortune 500 companies when it came to any one of several important measures —sales, profits, assets, or employment.

When we looked at market share along similar lines, we got an even bigger shock. After analyzing the numbers, we found we had a 6 percent share of the market that drove three-quarters of overall market demand. We had a 15 percent share of the segment that accounted for a quarter of demand. This proved how we had been marshaling our resources toward the wrong part of the market. In effect, we had been majoring in minors.

Finally, when we started examining the ways customers were actually using computers, we found that of the more than 100 major uses—applications software—for mid-range computers, 40 of them cinched the buying decision for about three-quarters of all customers.

We learned something else about customers and the way they used computers too. Our analysis showed three kinds of customers when you looked at them as users—those on the cutting edge, those in the middle, and those on the lagging end. For example, our team of industry experts identified certain school districts as cutting-edge customers. They held this distinction in our minds because we knew they wanted to do things such as connect the personal computers they used for classroom instruction to the mid-range computers they used for administrative purposes at their district central offices. This would allow a teacher to, say, record a student's absence by plunking a few keys and zipping it off electronically to school administrators, instead of hiking a sheet of paper to the principal's office. In wanting to achieve this capability, these districts had put themselves ahead of others by using computers in a way that will one day undoubtedly become commonplace.

We had to give primacy to appealing to such customers. The reason: Cutting-edge customers are the ones who lead a market to where it will ultimately evolve. Others will eventually follow. If we gave cutting-edge customers what they needed, we'd assure ourselves of giving the followers what they would soon need as well. We came to call these cutting-edge applications "mission critical"; we *had* to have them to assure our success in a given market.

You might say we segmented another aspect to the market too. Along with looking at customers and their needs, Tang also launched an initiative to dissect our competition in the mid-range market. We'd always done competitive analysis and IBM Rochester actually had been quite good at it. But we did only one facet of the job. Competitive analysis consisted of buying a competitor's machine and literally taking it apart to see how it ticked. (This is standard operating procedure throughout the computer industry.) But this approach is like looking at the competition through a rear-view mirror—we were only seeing where they'd been. In the escalating battle for the mid-range market, however, we also had to know where they were *going*—and why.

We did that by analyzing our competitors not just as products but as companies with certain strategic motivations. We collected everything we could on each of them —annual reports, Securities & Exchange Commission filings, and any other publicly available document. We bought reports from consultants and market analysts. This entailed another cross-functional effort. IBM Rochester business analysts and accounting types began looking at competitors in terms of market share, revenue growth, and other measures. We had technical people investigating how competitors developed their products and what tools they used. They found this information readily available in technical publications and articles. We tracked more than 250 different competitors in our market worldwide and all this information came together to give us a picture of competitors' business strategy, particularly *where they were headed*. We could begin to see where we could head them off at the pass.

Our analysis gave us some other insights too. We discovered that the 250 competitors could be bunched into a handful of different groups, each on a different part of the market. We also found that all competitors were not equal. Of the 250, six held more than 4 percent of the market each. Six others held 2-4 percent each. The rest had shares of less than 2 percent. This told us two things. One, we didn't have to compete with everyone, only our key competitors. We could even ally with some of the smaller ones. Two, we shouldn't have such an inferiority complex about ourselves in the mid-range. Yes, we'd lost market share.

But the numbers showed that we still ranked a strong number two.

Now, we were ready for the next critical step. We had learned from the failure of Fort Knox that we couldn't be all things to all people. We couldn't attack the market for mid-range computers with a shotgun, as we had done with our handful of incompatible machines. The market was just too broad. We had to focus and pick the places where we wanted to compete. We had to *target* certain markets.

Our work convinced us that, to sell a computer like Silverlake, we required more than just a superior machine. We saw four critical factors to success. One, we needed a superior machine, yes. But, two, and perhaps most critical, we needed the right kinds of applications software to run on it. Three, we needed sales channels and distribution to reach the right customers. And, four, we required strong customer support and service. If we could go into a market with all four of those "critical success factors," as we called them, chances were good we'd meet customer needs, beat the competition, and come away with a sale.

When we took these four factors into account, we found we could divide target markets into two groups—*natural markets* and *investment markets*. Natural markets were those where we had a "natural advantage" because we had the four critical success factors going for us. Investment markets were those where we needed to invest to get, create, or bolster the factors necessary for success. In dozens of desirable market segments, we lacked one or more success factors. The decision to go after natural markets was easy enough—no one disputed that we should play to our strengths. It really came down to choosing which investment markets we wanted to target. Collar's segmentation analysis gave us our answers. We picked those with the most promise, based on such factors as growth and demand.

By the end of our targeting process, Collar had his sights fixed on 17 major industry segments. We knew we wanted Silverlake to be a machine that would appeal to users in such businesses as insurance, distribution, health

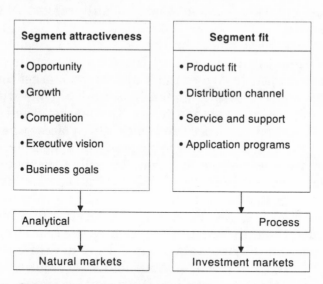

Figure 3. Selecting target markets

care, manufacturing and engineering, and state and local government, to name a few. According to one old adage, the three most important things in real estate are location, location, and location. Thanks to our segmenting and targeting effort, we had dealt with the three most important things to Silverlake's success—focus, focus, and focus.

To give Silverlake maximum appeal to our target markets, we had one final task to perform: how to *position* it against competing machines. Positioning is the process of giving a product certain benefits and attributes that make it distinctive *in the customer's mind*, thus setting it apart from the competition. In a perfect world, the job of positioning a product should be done before the product even goes into design. Unfortunately, because the timetable for creating Silverlake was so compressed and because we were dealing with a brand new planning approach, we didn't get to this phase ourselves until later in the Silverlake development cycle. So for us, positioning entailed articulating the attributes that would make Silverlake stand out in the crowd.

When we met to hash out Silverlake's position in the market, the planners marched in with a list of its special characteristics. From our needs and competitive analysis we felt we knew what benchmarks would make for a superior machine. And the planners had articulated those characteristics as they were coming to be embodied in Silverlake. But a problem existed. The planners had expressed Silverlake's chief characteristics in detailed technical terms, such as "single-level storage" and "externally described data." As they went down their list, it became apparent that we had once again lapsed into our old product-driven mentality. We were expressing our machine's features in terms that appealed to us as engineers, programmers, and technology nerds. We weren't expressing them in terms *that were most important to customers*.

Roy Bauer was sitting in the back of the room where we were discussing our positioning strategy and was taking it all in. Finally, he spoke up. He'd been thinking of our positioning in terms of his hobby—programming for small businesses. And the language we were using, he said, certainly wasn't going to connect with the people he knew who ran small businesses, people who could well be our customers. We had to start thinking about the Silverlake and its attributes from their perspective, not ours.

We realized that our initial go at positioning was tantamount to telling customers how we had designed Silverlake. But that was something that customers really didn't care about. All they wanted to know was what benefits Silverlake would offer them. Once we reminded ourselves of that, we could articulate and bunch all of Silverlake's capabilities in terms of five straightforward, concrete benefits. As we eventually expressed it, Silverlake offered customers:

• **Simplicity**. We had designed Silverlake so that a customer didn't need extensive expertise to use it. We created thousands of menus and help screens that would make it simple to use for even rank novices. For foreign customers, Silverlake's internal software would be in their native language. They didn't have to go through the trouble of translating software themselves—or waiting months for someone else to do it.

- **Solutions**. They'd find no dearth of applications programs to run on our machine, which had typically been the case in the past. All the programs that ran on the System/36 and System/38 predecessor machines would also run on Silverlake. Customers who owned those machines wouldn't have to watch their investment in software go down the drain if they wanted to switch to a Silverlake. We were also going to introduce Silverlake with some 1,000 applications ready for use and we made it capable of networking with other machines to a far higher degree than any of its predecessors.

- **Productivity**. Silverlake came with programming languages, tools, and utilities that allowed its owners to create software faster and with fewer programmers. As a standard feature, it was equipped with an integrated relational database, which allowed *all* information stored within it to be sorted and called up into pre-defined categories. Its design also gave it "artificial intelligence," a capability that enabled the computer to make time-saving judgment calls just as a human expert would.

- **Growth**. The Silverlake would be coming to market as a family of six models ranging from a very small system for $15,000 to a very large one for as much as $1 million. This span meant that the customer could get more power and capability as needs dictated. As they got bigger and more sophisticated, they wouldn't have to go through the trouble of switching to an entirely new system. Moreover, Silverlake offered some advanced technological capabilities the customer could grow into. It allowed customers to actually store images—a capability that will be coming into increasing use. For example, an insurance company could store in the computer pictures of autos involved in accident claims.

- **Support**. The Silverlake would actually go to customers with an "electronic classroom" inside. They would need to go no farther than the machine itself to learn how to use it. Through a feature we called "Electronic Customer Support," the machine's software could be updated, the machine itself diagnosed and repaired, just by hooking up with our technicians and their computers via telephone lines.

The benefits were clear—even to someone who didn't know a whit about computers. Perhaps more than anything, this positioning statement showed we'd made progress in becoming a market-driven company.

This whole approach to the market—segmenting, targeting, and positioning—was about to give us a huge payoff as we prepared to unveil Silverlake. We knew exactly who our customers were, who they could be, and what they needed. We knew this more completely and thoroughly than ever before and we knew what markets we wanted to pursue—that allowed us to tailor our machine for maximum appeal. It also permitted us to concentrate our resources, in terms of technology, marketing, and sales. With this information, we had the basis from which we could actually give our sales representatives the names and addresses of customers for whom Silverlake was perfectly suited. Once we got to them, we could tell them clearly and concisely what Silverlake could do for them.

Not bad for a bunch of hicks—not bad at all. And there was a broader lesson for others in what we did. Every enterprise needs to have an intimate relationship with its markets. It has to know everything about its customers —most of all, who they are, who they could be, and what they want. Given the propensity of markets and customers to change—swift change—failing to know your market risks falling out of touch with it. The danger in that is misjudging it, even missing it altogether.

But knowing a market can't be left to anecdote. Markets must be analyzed methodically, by breaking them down into their component parts. That also takes focus—not just to know markets, but to penetrate them. And that means picking and choosing. To penetrate them involves positioning a product in a way that distinctively sets it apart from its competition.

We succeeded in doing all that during the course of the Silverlake Project. Once we knew what our most promising markets would be and what our customers wanted, we had to get down to the hardest part. We had to start making choices—choices about what features and functions would best suit those customers and markets. And that brought us to the point of deciding how and where we wanted to spend our money—a matter that threatened to tear us apart by the bitter infighting it generated.

5

ALLOCATING RESOURCES BY SETTING PRIORITIES

We'll really know what we're doing when we can say NO.

—JIM CORAZA, Director of Advanced System Management,
IBM Rochester

The skirmishes started from day one. And then they kept mounting into what seemed like one long, unrelenting debate. The problem was that we were doing all that scrapping among ourselves, and the rivalry was threatening to slow work on the Silverlake Project to a grind.

The origins of the heated debates were engineering, programming, and marketing. And for the most part, they generated more heat than light. Each had their own strong-willed ideas about what the Silverlake should be able to do. But to give the Silverlake this feature or that function was going to take people, equipment, and other resources—money, in short. And it was money—the funding of the myriad pieces of the Silverlake Project—that became such a source of discord.

What made it even more frustrating was that everyone seemed to have a legitimate claim for funding ahead of someone else. But in reality, there just wasn't enough money to fulfill everyone's wish list. So we were faced with questions. How much money should go where? On what basis would we make allocations? Experience wasn't much help; none of us had ever been involved in anything so big and complex, so it was hard to rely on anything we'd previously learned. Would we depend on the proverbial "gut feel?" Hardly. Far too much was at stake to admit anything to intuition.

Our quandary was a quintessential one. Like so many enterprises, we had to cope with the untenable demands of satisfying virtually unlimited needs on a very limited budget. It was as though an immutable law of physics applied—for every action there is an equal and opposite reaction. No matter which way we came down, we could count on offending somebody, and the resulting ruckus was bound to take a toll on consensus, cooperation, and morale.

The real problem, though, was that each organization was evaluating and committing to their piece-parts with no real understanding of how their decisions were affecting the whole. And although we had a consolidation process for the piece-parts, *we were unable to convincingly demonstrate that the final result would balance the needs for market share, technology leadership, and for being affordable and competitive.* We had no methodical, objective basis for making these tradeoffs, *especially in a way that served our overall business objectives.* Consequently, we had trouble explaining our decisions to those affected or to those we answered to in a credible, defensible way. Indeed, for as rational as most managers want to be, when it comes to allocating resources, they frequently lack the methodologies for making systematic decisions. So they're forced to act by decree. Or whim. Or, worse, they wind up, like a practiced old Capitol Hill pol, making stopgap attempts at appeasing the sundry, and often competing, interests found in most organizations.

Making tradeoffs is a fact of organizational life, especially in an era of doing more with less. So priorities have to be set. But *those priorities must be determined on the basis of the enterprise's overall objectives.* Resource decisions need to be made, to borrow a New Age term, *holistically* —that is, with their consequences to the entire enterprise and all its parts in mind. Setting priorities—priorities that will serve as a guide to resource decisions—shouldn't be a matter of guesswork. It must be done through a process that's as systematic as possible. And one which produces repeatable results. This is precisely what we did—not only in allocating resources but, ultimately, in determining the shape of the entire Silverlake Project.

The battleground for our little war over resources was actually a three-inch thick printout called the "System Plan." Compiled by our planners as one of the first formal steps involved in the Silverlake Project, the System Plan detailed every one of the Silverlake's proposed functions and features. It outlined our plans for its memory size and speed, its data storage capacities, the terminals and printers it would accommodate, the programming languages it would run, the applications software it would operate, and more—everything about the machine. It consisted of some 2,000 engineering specifications. It also doubled as a budget document, with its 2,000 "specs" serving as "line items," each embodying the estimated cost of making the spec a reality.

Each line-item allocation could range from $100,000 to millions of dollars. But problems invariably arose, because the System Plan, like the federal budget, accounted for every penny available to us. Unlike the federal government, we couldn't engage in deficit spending.

Though we had a basic System Plan at the outset of a development project, it invariably changed as we went along. A new technology, an emerging customer need, a promising new market, a move by the competition—all gave us reason to change the System Plan at some point. But if we wanted to add a new feature or function to the plan, then the money to fund the addition had to come from somewhere else *within* the System Plan; it had to be at the expense of some other line item.

So one of two things happened. We wound up taking funds from everyone, right across the board. Or we'd simply cancel a part of the System Plan. Sometimes we'd even cross something right off in mid-course, sending millions of dollars in wasted efforts up in smoke. This not only increased costs, but saddled us with delays, which down the line never failed to translate into lost sales. But no matter what form it took, this give and take, as you might well imagine, caused no small amount of consternation, especially for those of us on the giving end.

We found ourselves facing the same unsavory situation as the Silverlake Project began moving forward from its System Plan. For example, as work progressed, it became apparent that desktop publishing was certain to become an important feature for the Silverlake to have. But adding this capability meant making a raft of inter-related changes to the System Plan. We'd have to come up with desktop publishing applications programs that would work on the machine. We'd have to make sure the Silverlake could accommodate video terminals and laser printers capable of the kind of high resolution needed to work with page layouts, pictures, graphs, and other illustrations. That was going to take the time and effort of engineers and programmers and whatever else they needed to bring this particular feature to fruition. And it was going to cost money, and the money was going to have to come from some other part of the project that already had been allocated.

Of course, when we began to suggest ways of freeing up the money, protests went ringing through the development lab. Perhaps we could curtail spending on some aspect of the hardware design that went into Silverlake's speed and performance. "What, and slow the machine down?" the engineers clamored in protest. "Are you crazy?" Well, then maybe we could delay equipping Silverlake with that new security feature that banks could use in connection with their automatic teller systems. "No way," sales and marketing would say. "We absolutely need that feature to sell into that market."

When it came right down it, the engineers and sales and marketing both had a point. But what were decision-makers, like Schwartz and Furey to do? They faced not only legitimate but compelling arguments from both sides and they had to choose. But how?

Victor Tang, who was in charge of planning, and Emilio Collar, who oversaw market analysis, watched as Furey, Schwartz, and other general managers struggled with such decisions. They figured there had to be a better way. They viewed this struggle as an issue fundamental to strategic decision making, one only compounded by the vast complexity of global markets. It simply begged for a more rigorous and systematic process. So together they embarked on an approach for setting priorities as the basis for allocating resources among the various—and often changing—line items in the System Plan. To their way of thinking, the only way to make sound decisions for allocating resources was to create a priority ranking for each and every one of the line items themselves. Those at the top of such a ranking would be given the most money first. Those at the bottom, well, they'd be expendable. If a new line item was required, it would be ranked and inserted in the right priority.

But what would be the basis for such a ranking? Markets? Technological considerations? Financial objectives? It actually had to be done on the basis of all three considerations. Not only that, we would have to take all three into account in a *balanced* way—one that would accomplish the broadest goals as well as the narrower business objectives of the Silverlake Project as a whole.

Setting priorities isn't difficult—as long as you relegate the ranking to a single criterion. If you want to buy a car with the lowest possible sticker price, ranking your options isn't that hard. You shop around, make a list of the sticker prices, note the lowest one compared to the others and there you have it. But what happens when you start taking other factors into consideration—fuel economy and maintenance costs, for instance? And to make it harder still, what if you consider subjective factors such as status and com-

fort? Suddenly, ranking your options becomes a very complicated affair, especially if you want to be thorough and
methodical.

All sorts of questions arise. What consideration should
be first and foremost? How much importance, or weight,
should you assign to each? Should sticker price account for
50 percent of your decision? Or 75? Or even 25? What about
comfort? Should it count for 5 percent or 85 percent? Other
factors start to emerge as well. What will be the car's
primary use? Is it a second car for the family or will it be
used for business? If you're a traveling salesperson, that
argues for one kind of car. If you're an on-site construction
engineer, that points to an entirely different one. What's
more, all these considerations are interdependent. They
create cross-impacts on each other. For instance, if you
want status and comfort, you inevitably have to be willing
to give something up on price and fuel economy.

Thankfully, Collar found a *model* for helping us make
our priority-setting decisions—a methodology to render the
ranking process more objective and systematic. It also
allowed us to take any number of criteria into consideration. In short, it enabled us to deal with our situation in
all its complexity. It was called the Analytical Hierarchical
Process (AHP), and was developed by Thomas Saaty, a professor at the University of Pittsburgh.

Saaty's AHP is a mathematically derived model and, as
such, allows its users to bring a degree of quantification to
what are ordinarily qualitative judgments. Fortunately,
however, you don't have to be a mathematician to use this
model. AHP gives decision making a structure, which looks
like a hierarchy. At the top is your goal. For the purposes of
illustration, we'll use the fairly simple, straightforward
example of buying a car. Below that, at the next level of
the hierarchy, comes the criteria by which you judge certain
options for reaching that goal. In buying a car, you might
consider such criteria as the sticker price, fuel economy,
maintenance costs, comfort, and even status. And finally, at
the bottom of the hierarchy are your options—say, Honda

Civic, Chrysler Caravan, Ford Taurus, Cadillac Seville, or Mercedes 560 SEL.

But as part of AHP, you, the decision maker, get to build the hierarchy. You establish the goal, the criteria, and the options. In so doing, you can actually bring ideas, anecdotal experience, even emotion into the process. While sticker price, fuel economy, and maintenance costs are all criteria that can be captured in concrete figures, comfort and status can't. Yet they can still become part of the deliberation. In creating the hierarchy, you get to attach a weight—a numerical expression of importance—to the criteria against which you score your options. If you assign fuel costs a higher relative importance than status, the process will lead you toward a much different car than if you ranked status over fuel economy. After you assign a weight to your criteria, you then begin to rate options, again by giving each one a weight. The result might be that, compared to a Mercedes, you will weigh a Civic higher for fuel economy than comfort.

Automated in the form of a relatively inexpensive software program called "Expert Choice," AHP is an extraordinarily powerful decision-making tool. It brings structure to decision making, yet it's flexible because you get to design a hierarchy of goals, criteria, and options customized to the particular problem at hand. It can be used with groups, and, as a collaborative effort, it can bring consensus to decision making. It allows you to quantify judgments, even subjective ones. *It also forces you to consider the interdependencies of your criteria to meet your goals.* AHP pinpoints for you where the impacts are highest or inconsistent. You can play "what-if" games with it: What if you regard comfort as your foremost consideration? What if instead, you consider fuel economy as the uppermost factor? AHP allows you to set priorities by taking several factors into consideration—factors that interplay and affect each other. In building the hierarchy, you can have goals and sub-goals. You can have several layers of criteria. You can also deal with several layers of options. In other words, you can address extraordinarily complex situations, ones with multi-dimensions that have interconnections every which way.

AHP became the template we imposed on our efforts to rank the line items of the System Plan so that we could earmark funds in a much more methodical, rationally defensible way. We began by getting together, a half dozen of the key executives involved in the Silverlake Project, including Schwartz and Furey.

In building our hierarchy, the first thing we needed to establish were our goals. Our main goal was to be the leader in the mid-range market, a declaration easy enough to make. But we had to go a level deeper. We needed to articulate specific and concrete business objectives for achieving these goals. Only then could we start setting priorities among system plan line items. It was really against those objectives that we would be making the hardnosed decisions about how much was to be spent where and on what. It didn't take the group long to agree that we had three main objectives: We wanted to increase market share, we wanted strong revenue growth, and we wanted to establish technological leadership in our markets.

Then we assigned a weight—a relative importance—to these goals. Weighted and ranked one way, these goals would have ended up in a business that looked one way. Ranked another, they would have created one utterly different. For example, if we gave market share priority over technology, we would try to make the Silverlake small and inexpensive, giving it as much appeal as possible to as many markets as we could. If, however, we ranked technological leadership over all else, we'd do just the opposite. We'd create big, expensive machines with all the bells and whistles. In short, if we were making cars, the way we ranked our goals would determine whether we were going to create something that looked closer to a Honda Civic or closer to a Mercedes 650 SEL.

Tang and Collar went around the room and got each executive to assign a weight to each one of these objectives and they asked them to discuss those weightings among themselves. They decided to first address the near-term priorities. Based on their weightings, our foremost business goal for the Silverlake was to generate as much revenue and profit as possible in the near term, which we defined as two to three years. This was understandable under the circumstances. The Silverlake was going to require a tremendous up-front investment by IBM—nearly $1 billion. We were on the defensive in the mid-range market. If we were to avoid disappointing IBM and the markets in general, the Silverlake would have to start racking up sales fast. That meant we'd have to de-emphasize, if not forego, some of the low-margin markets we'd have pursued in the cause of market share and some of the bells and whistles we'd have chased in the name of technological primacy. Our long-term investment strategies were the avenue for those markets and technologies. In the short term, we'd have to concentrate more on our "natural markets," leaving the pursuit of additional markets and penetration of "investment markets" as a longer-term strategy.

Now, we had our near-term goals ranked by their relative importance to us—revenues first, market share second, and technological leadership third. We were ready to start ranking options in three main ways, which would eventually serve as the basis for setting priorities and allocating resources for the System Plan. These three main ways involved markets, technologies, and financial objectives.

Because we were bent on becoming a market-driven organization, we knew that everything—everything—we did had to follow from what it would take to meet our customers' needs. But who were our customers? They were going to be in our chosen markets. So before we made any decisions about allocating resources to functions and features, we had to discern what customers were most important. To do that, we needed a priority ranking of our markets, consistent with our primary goal of generating revenues quickly.

Our segmenting work had given us a list of some 300 potential markets. Based on preliminary judgments, we considered 100 of them reasonable targets. But we had to

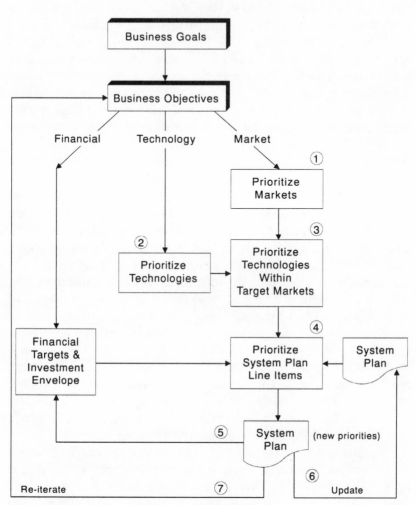

Figure 4. Strategic prioritization process

whittle the list even more. So we decided to rank these markets using the AHP template. We already had our goals. But to rank our markets, we had to establish criteria. We decided on two basic criteria. The first was market attractiveness in terms of such things as market growth, sales potential, and competitive intensity. The second was our ability to compete in terms of our four "critical success

90

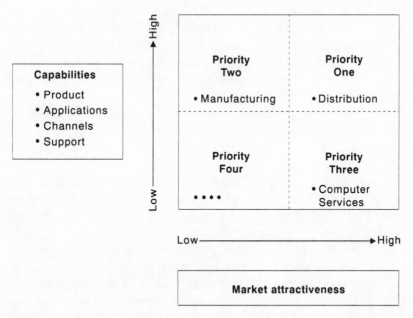

Figure 5. Market ranking

factors"—whether our machine would be right for a particular market, whether it came with the right software applications, whether we had the right marketing channels to
reach a market, and whether we had an infrastructure to
provide service and support. (Having these four factors
simply meant that we could offer our customers not just a
machine but a *complete solution* to satisfy their business
needs.)

Using AHP, we literally assigned a weight to each and
every market in comparison to each and every other
market. The criteria we applied included objective measures, such as growth rates, as well as subjective ones, such
as how well our offerings of software applications stood up
against the competition. Based on our goals, our weighted
criteria, our ratings of each option, it yielded a priority
ranking of markets. Distribution came out at the very top.
Although it wasn't the fastest growing market around, it

91

offered a stable source of revenues, we were already a leader in it with our System/36, and we had what it took to succeed: We had a highly regarded lineup of software applications, we had a sales force that knew the industry, and we had a field-service network in place to support it. Manufacturing came second, computer services third, hospitals fourth, and so on down the line.

We didn't stop there, of course. The next step was to rank the technology options and come up with a similar list. So we decided to rate technologies, again, on the basis of what boiled down to two criteria. One was technical attractiveness. Would it put us on the leading edge of certain uses in a given market? Could that feature or function be used in other markets? The second was our ability to develop it. Did we have the core competencies? Would we have to add people or develop new skills? We ranked each technology option by assigning it a numerical rating. Once again, based on our goals and our weighted criteria, we came up with a priority ranking of technologies. Communications standards, or giving Silverlake the ability to talk and work with other computers of a different make or model, came out near the top of our list, followed by technologies having to do with programming, networking, databases, graphics, and others.

We still weren't done. We needed to take another step. We had to understand the interdependencies among markets and technologies relative to investment criteria. We asked, What are the levels of investments for these markets with these technologies? What do these markets with these technologies yield in terms of cash flow, profits, and return on investment? We came up with yet a ranking that simultaneously considered the importance of markets and technologies in the context of investment criteria.

Now with this ranking of markets and technologies, we could get down, finally, to ranking the line items of the System Plan. We formed a *cross-functional team* of engineers, programmers, business planners, and marketers. They assessed each and every line item in the Silverlake

System Plan against our ranking of target markets and technologies.

Despite the sound of it, the process, like all models, had its limitations. In the numbers we didn't wind up with a cut-and-dried ranking of markets and technologies. In fact, for some options the numbers were so close as to be statistically insignificant. The situation is similar to Olympic scoring in gymnastics. The point spread among some athletes is so small that fractions of a point separate them in the rankings. That meant in some cases, we still had to make a judgment call.

Nevertheless, once we did that, once we knew which markets and technologies were most important—and in priority order—making those tough line-item tradeoffs became far less painful. Deciding became a matter of asking a few simple questions. What market will this line item serve? What technology? Where does that market or technology stand on our priority list? Line items related to markets and technologies higher on the list took precedence over those lower.

All this had very real consequences. In the past, we would sometimes chase markets simply because some highly placed executive decreed we should. Usually these decrees were based on an anecdotal experience with a particular customer or industry. But with our priority ranking in hand, it became easier to fend off such unjustified dictates. For example, someone came to us with a suggestion to adapt the Silverlake for use by intelligence agencies. Like everything else, spying has gone high-tech too. It's now possible to know what a computer is doing by using a remote "listening" device to pick up the electromagnetic impulses it emits. If we wanted to sell computers to this particular sector of the government market, we would have had to do quite a bit of re-engineering to make the machine secure against such eavesdropping. The decision was easy. Was that market on our priority list? No. So should we make the investment? Absolutely not. For the first time, we could confidently articulate what businesses we were in and,

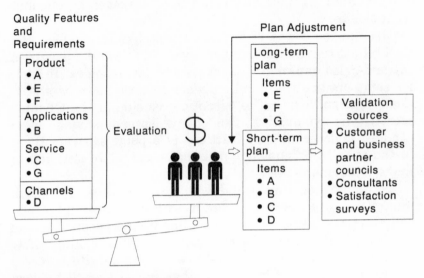

Figure 6. Prioritization process

more importantly, which ones we were not.

Having done this for the short term, we moved on to an analysis of longer-term priorities. There, market share became the dominant consideration.

We had come up with a process for setting priorities and, thus, for making decisions on earmarking resources. It's a rare organization that doesn't find itself in need of some similarly systematic process. In today's competitive global marketplace, where almost everyone is finding themselves having to do more with less, figuring how much money should be spent where may be one of a manager's most difficult tasks. But the problems and pain can be obviated by setting priorities. It's simple: Before you decide how to budget, you've simply got to know what's most important, especially in reaching your organization's overarching goals in a holistic, balanced way. As straightforward as that sounds, however, it's hardly a simple task. Making decisions today depends on taking into consideration any number of interdependent goals, criteria, and options. As we proved, though, relying on a model can make the job of setting priorities to allocate resources much more methodical and objective and, therefore, much more credible and defensible.

Such a process allowed to us to go so far as to rank the features and functions of the Silverlake, mostly in accordance with the markets that were most important to us. It also gave us a balanced and stable plan, which helped us achieve a shorter development cycle. With that, our transformation into a market-driven enterprise had taken another step forward. But the System Plan was just that, a plan. Now we had to get down to the real work—of turning our plans into an operating machine. We had less than two years to do that. So a single looming question now stood before us: How?

6

BREAKING THE TIME BARRIER

Miracles have to occur.

— JIM FLYNN, Manager of Advanced System Engineering, IBM Rochester

We could have played it safe and told corporate headquarters that doing so much in such a short time was a practical impossibility. We didn't. Instead we took this blind leap of faith. But when we committed to the Silverlake Project we didn't realize just how deep was the abyss into which we'd jumped. Not until we were well on our way down did we begin to fathom the sheer expanse of our effort. Silverlake was going to be of a magnitude *at least* three times bigger and more complex than any other computer project we'd undertaken. When this started to sink in, many of us began thinking we *should* have played it safe.

It was too late now. Besides, if Silverlake seemed undoable, our own ambitions for it were as much to blame as anything. We had, after all, set for ourselves the goal of creating not just an evolutionary new computer but a standard-setting one—with functions never before seen by our customers in a mid-range machine. In it we were going to combine our own incompatible System/36 and System/38 machines, which meant we were going to make Silverlake capable of running thousands of different applications programs that could work on one or the other, but not both, of its two predecessors.

Our plans also called for making Silverlake a family of models with a price-performance span vaster than any previous lines. The little one had to have the same basic architecture and functionality as the big one, just as if you could make a Cessna do the same work as a giant C-140 transport. Finally, the Silverlake was conceived as a *global* product and, as such, it was going to hit the market in at least 120 countries *all at the same time.*

When we began translating these lofty goals into the hard reality of actually getting the Silverlake built and into the market, we found ourselves confronting a feat of Promethean proportions. The hardware alone was to consist of more than 50,000 different parts—but even that number glossed over its colossal complexity. Like every computer, the Silverlake would work on the basis of the binary code, the language spoken in the form of electrical pulses carried along thousands and thousands of circuits contained on silicon chips no bigger than a fingernail. In a computer, each circuit performs a certain function, so each one is roughly analogous to the moving part in a machine of the more mechanical kind. And how many "moving parts" needed to be designed into the Silverlake? For the biggest model, as many as 2.5 million.

The numbers were even more incredible for the software. The Silverlake's most basic set of software instructions would consist of some *7 million* lines of code, which meant that, even at our improved programmer productivity rates, we were talking about 3,000 person-years of programming effort. Since every line of software code has a specific function, you can think of a line of code as a moving part too. So counting the circuitry and the basic software, we were

97

looking at an endeavor that was the equivalent of building a device with as many as *10 million* moving parts.

With the project taken in its totality, our job was even more complicated. Since we wanted to sell the machine worldwide, the Silverlake had to work in no less than 27 different national languages. We not only had to translate all our software that many times over, but we had to do the same for the 33,000 pages of operating instructions and any other documentation. To give the Silverlake the simultaneous worldwide launch we planned, we had to prepare three different factories—one in the United States, one in Europe, and one in Latin America—to manufacture it. We figured we had to train some 32,000 people to sell and service it in the 120 countries we'd targeted as markets.

But all this wasn't the real reason why the Silverlake Project loomed so immense and intimidating. The real challenge was this: We had to have it all done by August 1988—just 28 short months away from the start of our endeavor. We'd never developed a machine and introduced it to the market in so little time; it usually took four to five years. To meet our schedule we had to cut the time to develop the hardware alone by *an entire year*. We had to pare the programming cycle by a full *18 months*. And to make it all that much tougher on ourselves we were committed to doing it without adding people or lowering morale.

If we were going to pull it off, we had to accelerate our efforts to supersonic speeds. We had to *break time barriers*. But in facing this imperative we were hardly unique. In fact our predicament in the world of computers was quite metaphorical. For any modern enterprise, life in the Electronic Age has become imbued with the same microsecond pace that it takes for a pulse of electricity to zip around the circuits on a silicon chip. Technology mutates in the blink of an eye. Social, political and economic developments rush by in a blur. What customers need and want can change overnight, and competition is proliferating and intensifying at geometric rates. IBM used to be one of perhaps 100 competitors in the computer industry; by the late 1980s, we were one of *50,000*. As technology leapfrogs, as competition escalates, product cycles become more short-lived. Our mid-range computer lines typically would sell in the market-place for seven years or more. Now we're lucky if they'll sustain themselves for five; personal computers last in the market for less than two.

The upshot: No matter who you are, if you're small or even as big and influential as IBM, you've got to move faster. And not just in a straight line like a sprinter making the 100-yard dash. To react to change, circumstance and competition, you also have to be quicker, like a basketball point guard. Getting to market fast and, better yet, first is now viewed as one of *the* most essential hallmarks of the twenty-first-century enterprise. The notion of speed has even become a business concept unto itself. It's known as time-based competition. Indeed, a study by McKinsey & Co., showed it's a concept that goes right to the bottom line. McKinsey found that a company can lose as much as a third of its potential profits on a product introduced to the market only six months late.

At IBM Rochester, we succeeded in making the process for creating the Silverlake swifter *and* more flexible. We markedly compressed the cycle of taking the computer from concept to the marketplace. And we did so by reconceiving the process on the basis of a few straightforward concepts: *parallelism and getting it right the first time.*

We had no choice. The traditional way simply took too long, and the main reason was because it was so linear and sequential. We started the traditional process by having our planners articulate a list of customer requirements. They produced those requirements based on what they interpreted customers needed and wanted. These, in turn, generated a list of product specifications, or a System Plan, as long as 2,000-items, which formed the basis for hardware engineering and programming.

The engineers and programmers designed a machine according to those "specs." Their work included designing all the individual chips with their myriad circuitry plus the "architecture," or the system, that made the chips work together as the computer itself. They sent the designs to be made into a few actual chips, and when they got them back, they built a prototype machine. They tested the prototype for bugs; just this "bring-up" phase could take 12 months. They redesigned, reworked, and built another prototype. Only after completing this second pass at the hardware did they release the prototype to programming for work to begin on the software. At this point, manufacturing got a prototype too so it could start planning and preparing to make the computer in volume.

The process of creating the software was just as sequential. It resembled making piece-parts for an assembly line. Software worked at "machining" individual parts, and when enough of the separate pieces were completed toward the end of the process, it began bolting them together into a functioning whole. Not until then did we get a chance to see where the problems were. We had to remachine and reassemble, which always wreaked havoc on our completion schedules.

When we got near enough to the end of the development process, we called in marketing and sales, showed them the fruits of our labors, and sent them off to prepare for market introduction. We launched in the United States. Only then did the independent software houses that developed applications for our machines begin creating the applications programs that did the real work for our customers. Six months after initial launch we'd offer the machine to the rest of the world, and then, we geared up to make it abroad and have the software vendors translate their applications into various national languages.

As for quality, we took an *ex post facto* approach. We knew we couldn't avoid a certain number of defects, and we accepted this practical reality. We just grit our teeth and devised a rigorous testing process for the machines as they were coming off the manufacturing lines. The defects we found we fixed. But the rework cost us inordinate amounts of time—and money. This was the process we followed to create the System/36, the System/38, and every other computer out of IBM Rochester. We were like just about everyone else in American industry. Instead of defect prevention, we did defect detection.

For the Silverlake Project, this just wasn't going to work. When the sheer demands imposed on us by our ambitions and timetable forced us to re-examine the traditional process, we realized it was riddled with flaws. Because each next step had to await the one before, product development simply took too long. That much was obvious. What's more, this lengthiness led to other problems.

Because it took as long as five years, the customer requirements we compiled at the outset of the process inevitably changed. A new technological advance came along. The businesses within a key market took a different turn, demanding new uses. Competition came to the market with something that called for a reaction. The fact was, at the end of five years, the market the computer was conceived for was not the same one into which we were launching it. We typically planned for these market shifts by padding the schedule, which only stretched the timetable more. Then there were always those developments we never saw coming. We reacted as best we could by going back to rework our plans and designs. But going back is excruciatingly agonizing—tremendously expensive too. And delays have a way of cascading into longer and longer postponements. To endure this, you have to have a high tolerance for pain along with massive resources. But by the mid-1980s, we simply didn't have the stomach for absorbing such self-imposed punishment.

Implicit in our difficulties of dealing with market shifts was how we regarded our customers *during* the process. We simply paid insufficient attention to them. We thought of our customers at the *beginning* of the process when we were in the conceptualization and planning phase for a new machine, and we thought of them at the *end* when we wanted to make a sale. But in between we became woefully out of touch.

Functional rigidity also corrupted the process. The Silverlake Project depended crucially on planning, engineering, programming, finance, manufacturing, marketing, and sales. If any one of those let us down, the project would have been crippled. Yet instead of acting like integral parts to an integrated whole, the various functional organizations at IBM Rochester acted more like a loose confederation of fiefdoms, each surrounded by its own high ramparts. Planning threw its findings "over the wall" to engineering and manufacturing, which hoisted the product "over the wall" to marketing, and so on.

Crucial functions such as marketing, for example, didn't get involved until a machine was close to launch. So their preparations often resembled the chaotic rush of an unpracticed fire drill. Worse, some functions never got a chance to have a bearing early on so that they could put their particular expertise to issues such as market positioning or serviceability; both always suffered in the primacy of our technological conceit.

Communication and coordination all along the chain suffered too. In a way it was like the child's game in which you whisper a word into each other's ear around a circle. Invariably, the word whispered by the first child is never the one spoken aloud by the last. Distortions occurred through the development process too. It never failed that manufacturing found itself making engineering changes on its own in the cause of manufacturing efficiency and cost-effectiveness.

The development lab had primary responsibility for creating each new machine. Yet we depended crucially on other IBM operations from around the world. But we handled these dependencies with a top-down attitude—we expected them to act at our sole behest, to give us *what* we needed and *when* we needed it. We invariably failed to take into full enough account their circumstances or other commitments. As a result, someone, somewhere, always failed to come through, and, of course, we wound up saddled with yet another setback and delay.

There was plenty wrong with the way we dealt with quality too. Removing defects after the fact not only slowed everything down, it actually carried an onerous cost. It meant we had to devote precious capital to testing equipment and to all those inspectors. In the cause of practicality we found ourselves simply accepting certain defects; it would cost too much to get them all out. But two things were wrong with that approach. First, we found that the number of defects we found and corrected was directly proportional to the ones we *didn't* find. So we wound up with bugs beyond our own present level of acceptance. Second, and even worse, we created a mentality where everyone along the whole process had their own acceptable level of defects—and the defects just accumulated as the process moved along.

For Silverlake, we had to do something new. But what? IBM's culture actually conditioned us to the response we had to these circumstances. Many people think of IBM as a conservative, white-shirt kind of company, but when it comes to technology it has a history of taking enormous risks. And when we do it's not always evident exactly where we have to go or, more important, *how* we're going to get there. So we have this saying: "We're going to schedule inventions" to get us from here to there. What we mean is that there will be no waiting for the divine light of inspiration. If it takes inventing a new tool, technology, or process to get us where we want to go, well, that's just what we'll do.

This is precisely what we did: We reinvented the development process. We compressed it. First, we abandoned our sequential approach in favor of one that overlapped various stages of the project so we could pursue them *parallel* to each other. Second, instead of waiting to deal with defects after the fact, we decided to find and remove the glitches *from the design*. We made a commitment to get it right from the start.

We began with the hardware development phase. At this point, one of the gutsiest—if not one of the most pivotal—decisions in the entire Silverlake project was made. Jim Flynn, the hard-driving engineer who was heading up the hardware engineering effort for Silverlake, committed to making a stable prototype not in "two passes" as we had done before but in just one. He put his career and the

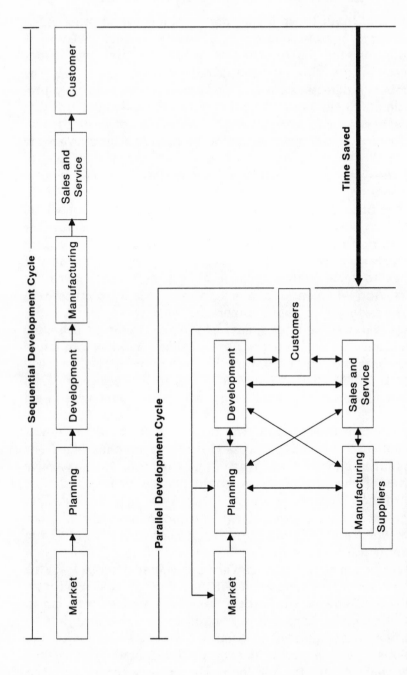

Figure 7. Sequential vs. parallel development

project on the line by making a promise to get the design right the first time.

Flynn bet on a technology known as computer simulation. Scientists are increasingly turning to simulation to test their most complex theories and complicated creations. Using mammoth programs that may run for days on the biggest and fastest computers in existence, they are essentially able to recreate an event and its effects in a make-believe world reconstructed within computer memory. With the computer taking into account the millions of variables involved in a real-life situation, they can, in effect, detonate a nuclear bomb inside the computer and then watch as the program predicts its effects on global weather patterns. Simulation as such is being used to predict everything from the effects of a new drug to the aerodynamics of new space-craft designs.

At IBM we had been using simulation for some time to recreate and test the workings of our chip designs. But the chips designed for a computer have to work *together*; that was the purpose of prototype testing—to see how they would operate once integrated into a computer system. What Flynn did was to take chip simulation a step further: He decided to simulate the entire computer system.

We did this by using a giant, one-of-a-kind IBM system, one custom made from several of our most powerful mainframes. This powerful super computer was called EVE, for Engineering Verification Engine. Flynn and his engineers entered Silverlake's overall system design, along with a set of performance specifications and standards. EVE simulated Silverlake's operation, showing us just how it would work and just as if it had been built out of silicon, wire, and metal. As it did, EVE pointed out the design flaws and glitches. After Flynn and his engineers reworked the design, they had chips made and assembled together into the circuit boards that made up Silverlake's central processing unit, the very brain of the computer itself.

Normally, the errant circuits that are found on such processor boards are rerouted by hand, using yellow wires. When we got to this point in the past, the back of a debugged board would look like a plate of spaghetti, with 300 or more wires stretching to and fro. But when we debugged Flynn's EVE-tested board, there were only six—*just six*—wires on the back. And the only reason we had those six is that they represented a newly added function untested by EVE.

In the past, debugging a system in its entirety usually took us as long as a whole year. But thanks to Flynn's EVE approach, we had a prototype of Silverlake up and running just *six* weeks after debugging began. By using EVE to *model* Silverlake's operation, we had shortened the development process by a full *10 months*.

Under our traditional approach, hardware engineering always built the working prototype, then turned it over to programming for work to begin on the system software. But for the Silverlake Project, *manufacturing* constructed the prototype. This did three things. First, it allowed engineering to focus its resources on refining Silverlake and designing the peripheral equipment that would go with it—printers, terminals, data storage devices, and such —without having to divert time and attention to building a prototype. Second, manufacturing, with its resources and expertise, quickly turned out not just one or two but *40* machines on which programming for Silverlake could begin. Third, it got manufacturing up the learning curve faster and off to a head start in gearing up to make the Silverlake *en masse*.

In keeping with its own commitments to parallelism, manufacturing brought to Rochester representatives from the various other IBM facilities around the world that would be contributing components or actually making the system for overseas markets.

Of course, giving our programmers a stable and reliable prototype so soon let them hit the ground running. Before Silverlake they had been relegated to paper planning and design until they could use an actual machine. Now a full 10 months ahead of time they could start creating those 7 million lines of code it would take to equip the Silverlake with its basic software.

106

That software, by the way, did not include the applications programs that did accounting, tracked inventory, recorded retail transactions or any of the thousands of other commercial tasks the Silverlake was to handle. The programming we were doing was for the operating system, along with several programming tools and "utilities" used for basic housecleaning functions. The operating system is the "traffic cop" from which all other software operates. Silverlake's operating system had to be unusually large because it had to be able to run applications created for both the incompatible System/36 and System/38. Plus we were integrating into the basic operating system functions that customers would normally have to purchase separately. These functions allowed the Silverlake to communicate with other computers over telephone lines, protect data against unauthorized access, and create databases from any and all of the information on it—all so automated that they required little intervention by the user.

Even though EVE had given work on this software such a head start, we still had to compress the programming cycle. So we reconceived it as well. We did this primarily by abandoning our old "piece-parts and assembly-line" approach. Instead, Dave Schleicher and his programmers broke the entire task into what they called "milestones." Each milestone consisted of one of Silverlake's major functions. And each was to be a freestanding, completely functional part of the whole. With this approach, we could very early on start booting up the software to see how it worked, adding milestone to milestone to create an ever bigger functioning whole. We could check the effectiveness and quality of our software code all along the way, instead of so near the very end. Another big advantage is that we could actually start showcasing our software to customers, not only to create interest but to garner their suggestions for improving it.

This approach to the programming work was like building a jetliner out on the runway. First, we built the landing gear. Then we constructed a fuselage as we pushed it up and down the tarmac. We added engines so that it could taxi itself. We put on a cockpit with the pilots inside to drive it toward a takeoff slot. We tacked on wings as it was about to go airborne. And then we added everything else while the jet was in the air, knowing that when we installed seats we could safely make a transatlantic flight filled with passengers.

The other innovation we brought to the process involved the way we tracked our progress. Under the old process, different managers assumed responsibility for different parts of the programming effort. If they got behind or ran into foul ups, they often kept it to themselves, hoping they could eventually work their way out. Aside from depending on their word, we had no objective way of telling whether work was on schedule. With the Silverlake, however, we set up a reporting and tracking system that updated progress each day.

We knew exactly where we stood and we tracked quality in the same daily way. We conducted test runs every day. (Toward the end we were putting up to a million lines of codes through their paces daily.) So on a day-to-day basis we counted the number of bugs we were finding in each and every kernel of our programming work and charted the numbers against a predictive defect-removal *model*. Managers couldn't cover up when the bugs began to mount to a threatening level. With nowhere to hide the errors, they didn't hesitate to call for help.

To give them that help, Schleicher established a special cadre of programmers. These were small groups dedicated solely to conducting rescue missions. We called them the "Bug Stompers," and they wore buttons with the international red-circle-with-a-slash sign for "no" superimposed over a drawing of an insect.

We deployed the Bug Stompers on several occasions. For instance, our plans for Silverlake called for putting an "electronic classroom" into the computer. A customer could learn how to use the Silverlake with the computer itself as teacher and tutor, on call and available whenever and for as long as its user, the "pupil", wanted. Work on the

Silverlake's self-instruction capability fell significantly behind. But thanks to the Bug Stompers we managed to have the classroom ready on time. If not for them, this extremely attractive feature would not have been available for as long as six months after we brought the Silverlake to market.

This kind of "concurrent engineering" has become one of the hot new approaches to product development and manufacturing, taking its place with such concepts as zero defects, cycle-time reduction, and just-in-time inventory control. But we didn't relegate our efforts at concurrency to just the hardware and software engineering phases of Silverlake's development. We went further. What we did was what you might call "concurrent product development." We extended concurrency to other parts of the product cycle as well. As a result, we got other phases of the process underway up to a year before we traditionally had.

For example, our efforts at targeting markets and positioning Silverlake were still underway 18 months before market introduction. By the end of 1987, every one of IBM's five geographically based business units—organizations for the United States, Canada, Europe, South America, and Asia-Pacific—were doing their own targeting analyses. Using the methods we had developed in planning, they were defining their own "natural" and "investment" markets. They calculated potential sales volumes, and they began to consider how best to reach their targets, whether by our own sales force or through some other channel of distribution. So by the time Silverlake was ready to be launched, nearly every IBM sales territory—from around the world —had marketing plans that were specific and concrete.

We also brought concurrency to the *worldwide* functions of manufacturing, marketing, finance, sales, and service. To do this and, again, to enhance coordination and communication on a global basis, we formed another *cross-functional* group. We called it the Project Management Team, or PMT for short. The idea came from Jim Coraza, who also headed it as the system manager, or the grand coordinator, for the entire Silverlake Project. The group, which came into being about midway to Silverlake's completion date, met once a month, usually in White Plains. It consisted of about 24 different Coraza-level managers. This included the manufacturing executives from our plants in Guadalajara, Mexico, and Santa Palomba, Italy, which would be joining IBM Rochester in building Silverlakes. It also counted among its members representatives from many of the 37 operations that would be contributing to the Silverlake—facilities that spanned the globe as well as the alphabet, from Atlanta, Georgia, to Yasu, Japan. Finally, it included top sales, finance, and service executives from each of IBM's five geographically based business units that covered the globe.

Through the PMT, we dealt early on not just with the logistics of worldwide manufacturing, but we hammered out the details to other crucial issues. For example, we got busy working on the matter of pricing the Silverlake in different countries. Pricing Silverlake for international sale was extremely tricky. We had to account for the differences in currency, economic circumstances, and the prices of competing machines in the many countries where we were going to offer it. But we couldn't create too much disparity for fear of encouraging cross-border buying. We didn't want customers from one country running to another to purchase our machine.

We began making real progress toward meeting our schedule, and it was never more visible than in a certain chart we kept. At the outset of the Silverlake Project, we prepared a chart illustrating our timetable. On the left side, at the very beginning, we listed the odds for success—1,000 to one. From left to right, we had listed each checkpoint we had to reach and *when*, in the seemingly impossible 28-month period. At each of these checkpoints we listed our odds, which kept coming down. Because we had compressed the process and saved so much rework by emphasizing quality during the development rather than only during the manufacturing cycle, we began to hit every checkpoint— *right on schedule.*

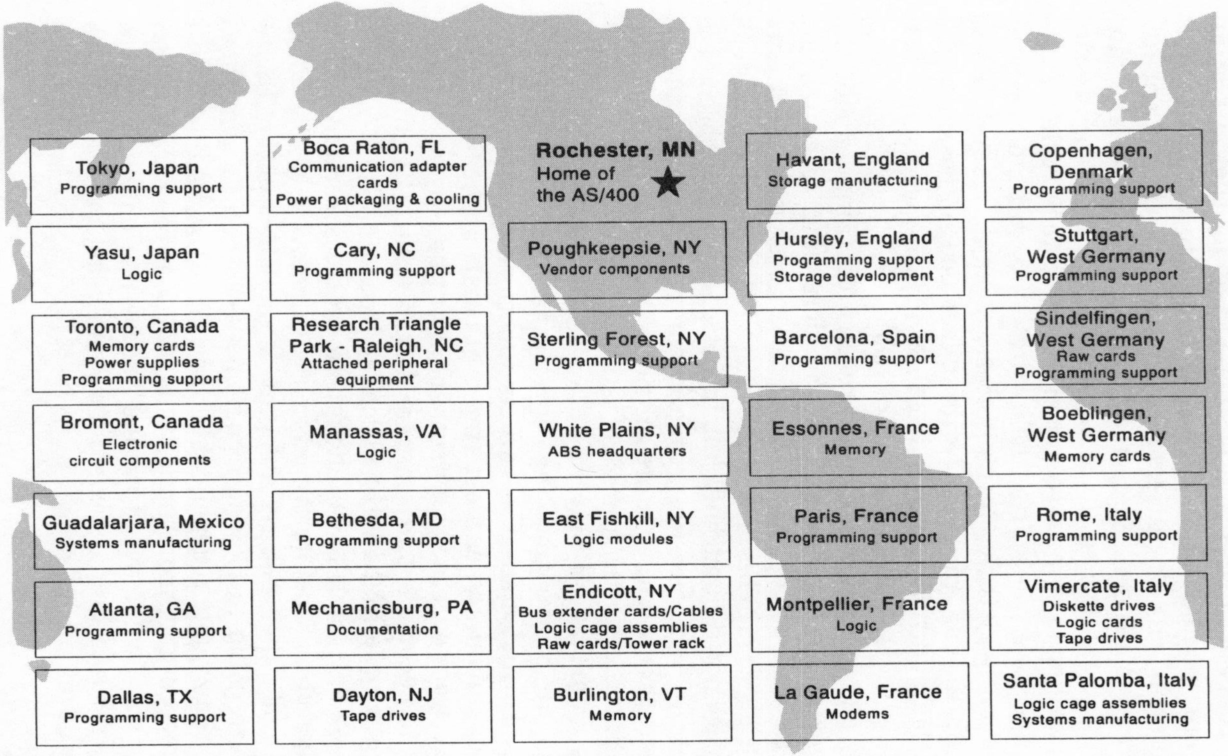

Tokyo, Japan
Programming support

Boca Raton, FL
Communication adapter cards
Power packaging & cooling

Rochester, MN
★
Home of the AS/400

Havant, England
Storage manufacturing

Copenhagen, Denmark
Programming support

Yasu, Japan
Logic

Cary, NC
Programming support

Poughkeepsie, NY
Vendor components

Hursley, England
Programming support
Storage development

Stuttgart, West Germany
Programming support

Toronto, Canada
Memory cards
Power supplies
Programming support

Research Triangle Park - Raleigh, NC
Attached peripheral equipment

Sterling Forest, NY
Programming support

Barcelona, Spain
Programming support

Sindelfingen, West Germany
Raw cards
Programming support

Bromont, Canada
Electronic circuit components

Manassas, VA
Logic

White Plains, NY
ABS headquarters

Essonnes, France
Memory

Boeblingen, West Germany
Memory cards

Guadalarjara, Mexico
Systems manufacturing

Bethesda, MD
Programming support

East Fishkill, NY
Logic modules

Paris, France
Programming support

Rome, Italy
Programming support

Atlanta, GA
Programming support

Mechanicsburg, PA
Documentation

Endicott, NY
Bus extender cards/Cables
Logic cage assemblies
Raw cards/Tower rack

Montpellier, France
Logic

Vimercate, Italy
Diskette drives
Logic cards
Tape drives

Dallas, TX
Programming support

Dayton, NJ
Tape drives

Burlington, VT
Memory

La Gaude, France
Modems

Santa Palomba, Italy
Logic cage assemblies
Systems manufacturing

Figure 8. AS/400 worldwide development and manufacturing

Then a remarkable thing began to happen. As we started to meet our schedule—and as we watched the odds for success get better and better—the doubt that characterized our mood at IBM Rochester began to subside. Before we knew it, our skepticism was supplanted with an entirely different attitude. We had bought into Silverlake and Furey's vision for us. This was *our* baby now. More important, we began to believe not only in our inevitable success for Silverlake, we started believing more and more in ourselves. Midway through the process, a can-do attitude began to suffuse our ranks. Nothing seemed impossible, not Silverlake and not Furey's dream of making us the market-driven standard bearer for all of IBM.

By our example, we'd also proven something—something instructional—for others. Time barriers have to be broken. And as we showed, they can indeed be shattered—in two essential ways. The first is to take on the various phases of a project not sequentially but in parallel. And the second is to get it right the first time. Remove defects in design; prevent them. It's far more efficient than having to rely on detecting them after a product is already made.

As smart as we may have looked in doing all this, our efforts at reinventing the development process still fell short. We had made the various functions of IBM partners with us during the earliest stages of creating the Silverlake. But we were still lacking another important ally. If we were going to become a truly market-driven enterprise, then our concept of quality had to be broader still.

It wasn't going to be enough to create a computer that was defect-free before we even manufactured it. We could have made the most reliable device anywhere, ever. But if we were going to wow our customers we had to give them more than just a dependable machine. We had to fulfill their needs and, more important, had to exceed their *expectations*. But what would it take? There was only one way to know. We had to make customers and other outsiders allies in the development process.

7

FORGING OUTSIDE PARTNERSHIPS

No way we can do it alone.

— DAVE SCHLEICHER, Director of Rochester Programming Center

We were bogged down in another big brouhaha. It was February 1987, a year into the Silverlake Project, and we simply couldn't agree. We just kept bumping heads and getting nowhere.

The battleground was the Rochester Management Board, our own IBM Rochester coordinating council. And the debate centered on a certain tape drive, a data-storage device. The question was whether we should make the System/38 tape drive work on Silverlake. But this also involved the whole issue of migration. From the outset, we had vowed to protect our customers' investment in their System/36 and System/38 machines by allowing them to migrate most of their existing software and peripheral equipment; data-storage devices, printers, network systems, communications gear. But how far could we really go?

Hundreds of different peripheral devices alone were used

on the System/36 and System/38. For each one we wanted to accommodate we had to create a special interface for the Silverlake. From an engineering and programming view point, this was a challenge tantamount to creating a compact disc player that could spin 45s and albums as well. And every device we obliged ourselves to migrate would not only consume precious time and resources, but affect overall system speed and performance as well. We didn't want to turn the Silverlake into a clunker by trying to make it do too much.

Even though we had a system design—an actual working prototype—we had to deal with thousands of unresolved questions like this as the Silverlake Project moved along. We faced a deluge of decisions, for example, about the innumerable ways users would interact with the Silverlake. How would we design the on-screen menus to convey the choices for executing this function or that? What would the accompanying "help screens" say? What would the menus look like? How many choices would we offer? To make it easier for the user, we could preset certain options, but which ones would become these default settings? We could design the keyboard so that a user could actuate an entire function by pressing a single key. But which functions? What keys? And where would they be located? That last question may sound elementary, but it can make a world of difference. For instance, we'd once put a "save" key right next to a "delete" key, and it doesn't take an engineering degree to figure the potential for calamity inherent in that design decision.

Few of these questions had such obvious answers as the "save-delete" design and the tape-drive issue was one. There were basically two positions in the tape-drive debate. Jim Flynn, the head of hardware engineering, argued that we had to migrate the tape drive; customers had shelled out $50,000 for each one and we simply couldn't expect them to eat such a big investment. On the other side, Dave Schleicher, the manager of programming, argued that the tape drive was outdated technology due soon for obsolescence and it just wasn't worth it to divert resources to bring it forward. Thus the dispute raged and for weeks we locked horns. Finally, in the midst of one particularly contentious session, Tom Furey raised his hand for silence.

"We're trying to make this decision on behalf of our customers, and the bottom line is that it's what *they* want, not what *we* want for them," he said. "We don't know what they really want, we just don't know, so we can't make this decision."

"Why don't we get some customers in here to ask them what *they* want us to do?"

With that simple suggestion, we embarked on a radically new way of doing things—a way that was to emerge as one of the most significant initiatives we took during the course of the Silverlake Project. Furey's recommendation would lead to a transformation in our honor-bound traditions of self-reliance and secrecy in the creation of *any* new machine at IBM Rochester. In its pursuit, we would make literally thousands of customers, independent software vendors and resellers, and other outsiders all co-developers with us in the Silverlake Project.

There was a time when companies did it all themselves. Going back to the emergence of mighty enterprises such as United States Steel Corporation and the iron ore and coal mines, barge lines, railroads, and mills it eventually owned, vertical integration became one of *the* prevailing hallmarks of the modern corporation. At IBM we engaged in every phase of making computers; we invented, designed, and manufactured them and most of their component parts, and then we shipped, sold, and serviced them ourselves. And we did this in markets all over the world. But no enterprise can go it alone any longer—the world is too complex and fast-changing.

No one has the resources—the manpower or money—to compete on a global scale in a broad spectrum of the markets. Furthermore, no enterprise, by itself, can bring to the table all the ingredients it takes to succeed in today's diverse, dynamic, and volatile markets. In our own case, we knew we just weren't selling computers anymore. We were selling solutions. So we knew it would take more than just a great machine. We also had to make good on three other critical success factors—applications, channels of distribution, and support services. But if we wanted to offer customers a complete solution to their data-processing needs, we had to have help. There was no way we could write the applications software for the thousands of tasks its users would want the Silverlake to perform. Nor could we rely on ourselves to sell and distribute in the multiplicity of markets we wanted to target. Nor could we, alone, support and service the hundreds of thousands of machines we aspired to sell around the world.

It's also no longer enough to meet customers' needs and expectations. You have to *exceed* them. In fact, you've got to anticipate and surpass them *going into the future*. Customers expect your product to help them get where they're *going*. In short, you have to become a *strategic* partner. But to do that, you've got to let them become a partner to you. To know and provide what they need five or 10 years from now, you have to invite them in as a full-fledged ally in what you're trying to do. You must *forge outside partnerships*, not just with customers but with suppliers, resellers, companies that make add-on or complementary products to your own, and, sometimes, even competitors.

Before the Silverlake Project, we were anything but open to outsiders. We were Fortress Rochester, and the symbols of our introversion were as plain to see as the buildings in which we kept ourselves. The shiny blue steel and tinted glass facade to our facility gives it a certain impenetrably encased appearance. The windows don't open. The cul-de-sac outside the main lobby entrance is lined with a series of what look to be decorative hitching posts. They're not: they're solid concrete pillars sunk 12 feet into the ground to prevent anyone from crashing a car into the building. Inside the lobby, the receptionists sit sealed off behind a wall of bullet proof glass. No one gets in without a badge and employees must pass theirs through electronic readers.

These are all prudent precautions, of course. But they also said something about our culture—and especially about the way we developed a new computer. Even in an innocent little town like Rochester, Minnesota, we insisted on wrapping ourselves in a cloak of security and secrecy that rivaled the precautions of an intelligence agency. When we decided to create a new machine, we were nothing if not tight-lipped. Sure, we'd have contact with outsiders but only in the most circumspect ways. If we discussed product plans or business strategies, we would insist on agreements that would prevent disclosure of information. And we would limit the number of customers with whom we would do this to be doubly safe. During the planning phase we'd invite a few customers in to talk in general and often vague terms about what we had in mind or we'd have planners visit customers. But that was just about it for much of the four or five years we took to bring a computer into being.

Aside from the top executives overseeing us, no one outside the development lab, not even our own sales and support people out in the field, was to know anything about the product until it was nearly ready for introduction. As we got close to unveiling the new machine, we'd send a few early versions to IBM field offices where they would undergo testing in something akin to real-world conditions. We might even let a handful of customers run the new machine through its paces. But all we were looking for at that point was a way to shake out the little bugs. The basic machine and its functions were set. What we had was what the market was going to get.

We seldom invited outsiders in because we thought we didn't have to. As we saw it, we were like a big store in a little town. Everyone in town came through our doors. Because we knew everyone as neighbors, we figured to know what they liked and wanted. And that's the way it was for us in our segment of the computer market. In the past, that is. In the early days of computing, when most customers were neophytes to this wonderful new technology, we probably knew more about how they could use a machine than they did. Plus, in the days when multimillion dollar mainframes accounted for most of the market, it wasn't hard for us to know our customers and know them well. They were the handful of top executives at big companies who had to sign off on such sizable capital investments. In terms of dollars, our market was huge; in terms of customers, though, it was, well, like living in a little town.

We had reasons for being so security conscious too. During the 1960s, IBM was sued for unfair trade practices. Some competitors accused us of touting machines still in development, of telling customers that we had some advanced new machine right around the corner—one that could make competing machines outdated, and thus discouraging customers from buying a non-IBM computer. As a legal and ethical precaution, we were forbidden from disclosing anything about a development project to anyone who didn't have an absolute need to know. We were forced into an even higher state of security by the seemingly persistent theft of our trade secrets too. In fact, during the early 1980s, we sued one of our competitors for stealing a proprietary software system. They had somehow gotten hold of the highly confidential specifications for the "operating system" in one of IBM's most successful mainframes. As a result, IBM, requires its employees to adhere to strict security measures. In fact, IBMers are actually evaluated on how well they follow these security strictures, including a "clean desk policy" that requires everything that is confidential to be put away under lock and key at the end of every day.

All this was well and good. But it began to have a counter productive effect. By keeping the world at bay, we began to lose touch with a market that was, to make matters even worse, changing on us. As computers came down in price, as they began to proliferate into all realms of life, as they began to lose their mystique to even school children, buying a computer no longer became a capital expenditure or a decision requiring approval by an exclusive club of headquarters executives. Especially when it came to the mid-sized computers we made, departments and branch office locations started making their own buying decisions. So these locations became our customers, along with the exploding numbers of small to medium businesses. In short, our once small universe of customers became innumerable. We couldn't keep track of who they were, let alone what they really needed.

If our disconnectedness didn't begin to dawn on us, IBM chairman John Akers would bring the point home. Twice a year, IBM holds a strategic planning conference involving the top 20 or so executives of the corporation. For two or three days, these officers hear from a procession of executives, mostly operating ones, about market conditions and business unit strategies. These are highly confidential affairs. But in 1986, in one of his first acts as chairman and chief executive, Akers invited representatives from six of our customers from around the world to sit in on the proceedings. He also asked the customers to address the group. Their main message: IBM wasn't heeding—wasn't listening to—its customers nearly enough. *Think*, our company magazine, described what Akers did—and what customers said —in a long article read with great interest by many of us.

Even if we hadn't gotten so indifferent to our customers, we had become too dependent on others to keep so much to ourselves anyway. By the mid-1980s, our own sales force —our IBM "blue suits" as we called them—accounted for only 40 percent of System/36 and System/38 global sales. The majority of our machines were being sold and serviced by what are known in the computer industry as "value-added resellers". We called them Business Partners, because we'd often enter into special contractual or business arrangements with them, including offering them discounts. This concept was widely practiced in IBM Italy during the early 1980s and was so successful we decided to adopt it worldwide.

In many cases, these independents would take one of our machines, load it with their own software, and sell it as a turnkey system—a billing and reservation system for small innkeepers, say. As a result, our machines found their way into hundreds of niche markets we couldn't cost-effectively pursue ourselves. Along with specializing in some industry segment, Business Partners also generally serviced a geo-

119

graphical territory. Our Business Partners actually became indispensable and accounted for more sales than our own IBM "blue suits." They also represented two of our four critical success factors. Not only did they create the applications software—the solutions—that made our computers a requisite part of doing business, but we counted on them to provide us with a cost-effective sales channel for reaching certain parts of our market.

Against this background, we went into the Silverlake Project. But as we got into it, the sheer demands of our tight timetable also forced us to question our fortress mentality. With only 28 months to get Silverlake to market, we had to make sure we were *getting things right the first time*, that we were, in fact, giving customers what they wanted. But how were we to know? We'd gotten burned, after all, just a few years before when we came to market with a package that put the System/36 to certain office uses—word-processing, document filing, electronic mail, and the like. We introduced it without getting customers to assess it first. It was slow and clunky, the market was disappointed, and we suffered embarrassment. With so much more riding on the Silverlake, we didn't want the same thing to happen. We also had to make certain that the customer requirements Silverlake was meant to satisfy weren't changing along the way. If they did, we wanted to be able to correct course, and on a dime. There'd be no time to go back and redesign if the market swerved on us before we could see it coming.

We knew we absolutely had to come to market with all the critical success factors in place—and on a *global scale*. Along with the Silverlake, applications, distribution, service, and support all had to be ready to go worldwide *at launch*, not a day later. To fall short on any one of those success factors would have meant we would have failed to meet customer expectations and would have made ourselves all that much more vulnerable to the competition. Plus, we'd seen this happen before: A machine hits the market without enough applications, say. Sales got off to a slow start. When sales start out slowly, customers, then the trade press, and then the market at large begin to question the viability of the machine. Then a vicious cycle begins. The bad press leads to slower sales, which leads to more bad press, and even slower sales, and so on until the machine literally winds up in a death spiral.

And so, we decided there was no option. We had to open the windows, metaphorically speaking, at IBM Rochester. So we broke with the past and began to let outsiders in.

Our first small step came in August 1986, just six months into the Silverlake Project. We had to know how well the Silverlake would run applications from the System/36 and System/38. Programming leader Dave Schleicher took the initiative to give a newly minted prototype machine to one of our Business Partners, Marcam Associates of Boston. Marcam had developed a highly regarded line of applications for small manufacturing companies; their portfolio included software for tasks such as inventory control, order entry, manufacturing requirements planning, logistics planning, and accounts receivable. For years Marcam had been adapting its applications for use on the System/36 and System/38. Through our systems engineers in Boston, we had close ties and a good relationship with Marcam. If anyone could gauge Silverlake's ability to cope with System/36 and System/38 software, Marcam could.

We also recruited Marcam's help out of sheer practical necessity. With the thousands of applications out there that had to be migrated, we seriously questioned whether we could afford the time, or the money, to test the compatibility of even a cross section. The challenge was daunting. So Schleicher concluded that if we were going to make sure the Silverlake could run all the software that our customers had spent billions of dollars to either create or buy, then, we had to depend on the good graces and resources of our customers and Business Partners to take on some of this crucial verification work.

Marcam's involvement brought an immediate payoff. They told us that migrating System/36 and System/38 applications over to the Silverlake had to be made easier.

121

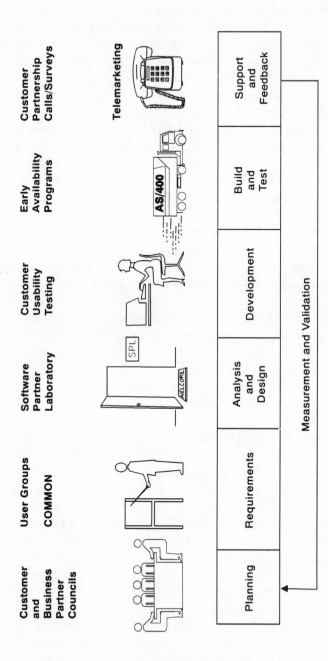

Figure 9. Customers involved

Marcam found that parts of its existing applications actually needed to be rewritten to make the conversion. But with Marcam's advice and suggestions, we developed ways to almost completely automate the conversion process. Marcam also gave us common sense suggestions for making our instruction manuals easier to understand.

Indeed, just a few months after this very first effort at letting outsiders in, we found ourselves embroiled in the knock-down, drag-out debate over the tape drive. Furey made the suggestion that we turn to those who really knew best, our customers. But as we took his words to heart, it became clear that the tape drive wasn't the only issue on which we needed to consult prospective Silverlake users. When we thought about it, we had a raft of questions begging for some answers from our customers.

We also realized something else. Our own programmers and engineers at work in the nooks and crannies of IBM Rochester just weren't equipped to make certain decisions about the way the Silverlake would perform in the hands of its users. Even with all their technical sophistication, they didn't have the hands-on experience of using a computer for billing guests at a New England inn, for knocking out the payroll in a school district office, for tracking inventory on a factory floor, or any of the other multitudinous real-life tasks the Silverlake would eventually be asked to do. Customers, however, would. They were the ones doing those tasks. Who better to tell us what worked and what didn't? So we took Furey's idea even further. We decided to invite several customers to IBM Rochester for a "council," a two-day meeting to fill them in on the Silverlake Project and hear what they had to say about what we were doing.

This was not an easy decision—even as much as we wanted to make it. There were major issues to consider, and we had grand debates when we tried to deal with them. We had to confront several questions. What about disclosure? Could we really trust our customers not to breach our confidence? How many people could we invite without completely compromising ourselves to the competition? We also faced

123

bureaucratic barriers. Those we invited would have to sign non-disclosure agreements, but corporate policy required us to get a special approval for each and every one. Not only that but policy set limits on the number of non-disclosure agreements we were allowed to enter, and we found ourselves pressing against that ceiling. These considerations caused no undue amount of stress.

Nevertheless, we resolved these issues and went ahead. Our first "customer council" convened. We invited two representatives from each of a dozen companies who had been loyal users of our System/36 and System/38 machines. Represented were small users, such as the John E. Schriver Co., an accounting firm from Cincinnati, Ohio; medium-sized users such as Farm Fresh, a dairy products distributor headquartered in Ponca City, Oklahoma; and big users, such as Merck & Company, the pharmaceuticals company of Rahway, New Jersey. We also hosted customers from a variety of industries, including Gannett Publishing of Arlington, Virginia, which publishes *USA Today*, Bass Pro Shops, the sporting goods catalogue company from Springfield, Missouri, Bally's, the casino company out of Atlantic City, New Jersey, and Caterpillar Tractor Inc. of Moline, Illinois. We had international users represented too, including Jefferson Smurfit, the big paper products manufacturer from Dublin, Ireland.

Day one of our confab belonged to us. We spent the morning briefing these customers on the hardware design for Silverlake. In the afternoon, we described its software. We told them how many models we would introduce and about the advanced functions Silverlake would perform. We talked about migration. We even discussed tentative pricing approaches and early thinking for purchase and leasing terms. We spared no detail. We told them as much as we thought they wanted to hear—and more. They were astonished. And for awhile they didn't exactly know what to do. One of our customers told us it was like being on a first date.

In the question-and-answer exchanges that followed, we began to encounter a persistent difficulty. We were having trouble understanding each other, not for any lack of cooperation or good faith but because we were talking a different language. The years we'd devoted to being a product-driven enterprise had left us speaking in a different dialect, if not a different tongue altogether, rather than the one our customers understood. We spoke in the language of engineers, in phrases peppered with technical specifications and the internal workings of our machine. But our customers wanted to speak in the language of day-to-day business. They wanted to talk in terms of the benefits a new machine could offer—doing things such as accounting, inventory control, order processing, manufacturing planning, and so on. It all only served to remind us how distant we had become from understanding our customers' real interests.

Day two belonged to them. They broke into small work groups and spent the morning formulating a reaction to what we'd told them. It was clear that they felt honored that we would consult them because they took to their task with a striking seriousness. In the afternoon, they gave what we were looking for: They reported their findings—a melange of reactions, suggestions, and substantive new ideas.

To our relief, they told us we were on the right track. They said they definitely wanted us to make it so that the Silverlake could use the System/38 tape drive. How could we say we wanted to protect their investment by making the Silverlake compatible with its predecessor machines and even think to do otherwise? They even came back at us on matters we hadn't dreamed they'd address. For example, they said they wanted us to look at simplifying doing business with us. One customer stood up to say how irked he was to write checks for three separate bills from IBM each month—one for the System/36 he leased, one for the software, and one for his service contract. Instead of three separate invoices, he said, why not make life easier by combining it all into one. It made sense to us too, and we marked the idea down for implementation.

In our eyes, the council was an unqualified success. We

learned a lot. We impressed our customers. They kept our confidence; there wasn't a single serious leak. We were so pleased we quickly followed this first council with others. We began convening a council in Rochester about once a quarter. We also organized councils in Europe and Japan. We put together similar gatherings for our Business Partners too. They were just as rewarding as the first. We learned from councils in Europe how critically important it was for us to offer a small entry-level Silverlake model. From Japan, we discovered how essential it was for us to *position* the Silverlake for that market by giving it advanced, never-before-seen features. This brought home to us that one of the realities of doing business on a global scale is that every market has its idiosyncrasies. For example, the Japanese prefer to buy something that is highly differentiated, offering unique value—one of the reasons why our own System/38 did well there.

We didn't send out invitations by whim either. Instead, we appointed a task force to assess and select those who should be brought into the development process. Using our market *segmentation* analysis, the task force made sure we picked leading-edge customers from the natural and investment markets we had *targeted* for Silverlake sales. By the time the Silverlake was ready for introduction, we had in-depth, back-and-forth exchanges with customers and Business Partners representing more than 4,500 firms from dozens of industries worldwide using over 12,000 systems.

We reaped a virtual bumper crop of benefits. They made sure we knew what product and service requirements were important to them. They advised us how to design our help screens and menus for optimal ease of use. We had always planned to equip the Silverlake with a special capability that would allow us to provide software updates and diagnose, even repair, the machine by connecting into it via phone lines. In response to a suggestion that came out of the Business Partner councils, we expanded this capability so that the independent software developers could provide the same type of support to their customers. By giving them this special advantage in the marketplace, we gave ourselves an extra one too.

With help from the councils, we were also able to address the often intractable problem of pricing. On all of our computers, the operating software was priced, and licensed, as an item separate from the hardware. For the Silverlake the operating software used on the largest model would be the same as that used on the smallest. But would it fair to license the software at a single price? Small-model users would be paying for capabilities they didn't have the capacity to use with their small machines. We could cut back capability to make it more affordable, but where would that leave the big-model users who wanted every bell and whistle? Or if we did, would we be building sources of incompatibilities for growth? In the end, our customers suggested pricing the software according to the size of the machine on which it was to be used, a solution that made everybody happy.

In addition to the councils, we began to involve outsiders in other ways too. Our alliance with Marcam showed us how we could rely on others to assume some of the verification work associated with migration. Marcam helped to assure us that *its* System/36 and System/38 programs would run on the Silverlake. But that wasn't enough. There were thousands of applications out there that had to be adapted to the Silverlake. These application programs needed to be prepared and, in some cases, even rewritten a bit so they could be understood by the Silverlake. If we wanted to have an attractive array of applications ready to use on the Silverlake at its launch, then the sooner we got started at migration the better.

To encourage our customers and business partners to begin this process, we decided to hold a special event. Actually, it was really a whole process that became an embedded part of the development cycle. We called it the "Migration Invitational." The idea was to invite customers and our Business Partners to Rochester—at our expense —to spend anywhere from two days to three weeks on a prototype machine converting their applications for use on Silverlake. This was one of those win-win ideas. For their part, customers got applications ready to use on an advanced machine, the Silverlake, even before it hit the market. For ours, we got to learn yet more about making the conversion process as painless as possible.

Like the councils, the invitational was such a success that it went on until we launched the Silverlake. We expanded the program to sites in Japan, Europe, Canada, and Latin America. By the time Silverlake was ready to hit the market, more than 175 customers and Business Partners had participated. These included users such as Chemical Bank, Baxter Health Care, Arthur Andersen, Campbell Soup, Volkswagen of America, Toyota U.S.A., the City of Los Angeles, and the German Federal Railroad. Our invitational resulted in the conversion of some 2,500 applications encompassing more than 200,000 programs and 70 million lines of code for use on our new machine.

To support these activities, which required Silverlake prototypes and no small amount of assistance from us, Schliecher created what he called the Software Partners Laboratory. Customers and Business Partners participating in the Migration Invitational used this facility. But it also became an important training venue. We staffed it with our own systems engineers, programmers, and marketing representatives from the field, providing them with valuable hands on experience with the Silverlake—well before it ever came to market.

We didn't restrict our migration efforts to existing customers and applications. We wanted the *best* applications to be ready to run on the Silverlake whether they were already used on one of our machines or not. We appointed a group to identify these top-of-the-line applications. We asked the creators of this software to work with us to migrate their applications to the Silverlake, and we agreed to help them however we could. Based on the segmenting, targeting and positioning work we'd done, we even went after software developers who had created leading applications for competing machines. This included AIS Corporation, which had created a highly regarded application for small medical practices that only worked on a mid-sized computer made by one of our competitors.

In addition to having a larder of applications ready for use even *before* Silverlake's market introduction, we gained other key benefits. We had hundreds of our systems engineers from out in the field help with the migrations. So when launch time arrived, they had the expertise to provide the competent service and support we saw as essential to Silverlake's success. Nine of our field engineers became so practiced on the Silverlake that they actually took on the task of training and educating other support personnel. They not only created educational materials, but they taught 28 courses to 1,000 of our people around the globe. Another major benefit was the early feedback the systems developers obtained directly from our customers. In the past, it would have taken months to produce a fix or enhancements as they worked their way through the company. With this process, software developers responded with fixes in days or weeks, and many, in minutes.

From the beginning, our ambition was to make Silverlake more than a replacement machine, one on which existing customers would simply switch existing applications. We wanted to expand our market and become our industry's undisputed leader. To do that we had to win new customers. To woo new customers, we had to come up with some new uses for the Silverlake. But what amazing new things would we make it do?

It came down to thinking of the Silverlake as more than a computer. It was really an *information* processor. And information comes in other forms besides the words and numbers that appear on the computer screen. Information comes to us in images, such as photos, and it arrives in the form of sound, such as the spoken word. So that it could deal with information in these other guises we decided to imbue Silverlake with two advanced applications. The first would give it the capability to store and retrieve images like photos or Xrays. The second would allow it to work in conjunction with the telephone.

The technology for both advanced applications already existed in one form or another. With its Rolm subsidiary, the maker of telephone equipment, IBM had been working on ways to unite the telephone and computer. But we didn't have all the pieces, or the time, to give the Silverlake these advanced characteristics all on our own. So we did it by striking partnerships.

The task for endowing Silverlake with the advanced applications of image and telephony, as we called them, belonged to a special Advanced Applications Group attached to Vic Tang's strategic planning organization. The organization combined the expertise of long-range planning with leading technology wizards to pinpoint and develop advances with the potential for becoming commercial breakthroughs. It was a *cross-functional* team consisting of about 80 programmers, engineers, marketers, and planners. To lead what was essentially another "skunk works"—one similar to the group that originally conceived the Silverlake—Furey tabbed a longtime IBM Rochester technology maven, Al Cutaia.

Over the years, Cutaia had established a genius for adapting technology to commercial uses. He was the one, for instance, who first took the technology of recording computer data on a magnetically-coated polymer "floppy disk" and used it as an input and output device for a computer system. For this accomplishment and many others, Cutaia eventually became an IBM Fellow, the first person at IBM Rochester to win the company's equivalent of the Nobel Prize. Not only did Cutaia know how to bring technology into our everyday lives, he was also relentless, famous for subtly needling away at the system, his superiors, and opponents to win a point or complete a task. Dealing with Cutaia, everybody said, was like being pecked to death by a duck.

Since our resources were stretched to the limit by our ambitions and our timetable for Silverlake, Cutaia's group worked on a shoestring budget. It also faced some degree of animosity from the main bodies of hardware engineers and software programmers. There was a feeling among them

130

that they were scrambling just to get the basics done by our 1988 deadline, while Cutaia and his people were off "tinkering with technological toys." Cutaia, however, was not to be deterred. When he couldn't get cooperation, technology, or software from within IBM, he went outside.

To give Silverlake its image-processing capability, Cutaia hooked up with a small Kalamazoo, Michigan, company called INET Inc. INET had already come up with a couple of successful applications for image technology. One of them was for real estate firms. With INET's system, a realtor could store photos of the various homes it had for sale as electronically retrievable images from a bank of laser-read optical disks (akin to the compact disks increasingly replacing music albums.) By punching in a few of the characteristics a client had in mind, the computer would compile a list of possible homes and their photos displayed right on the computer screen. Instead of driving clients from home to home to home, a realtor could conduct a tour without ever leaving the office.

INET adapted its technology for use on a Silverlake. Then Cutaia found a way to see how well it worked—and to refine it—in a real-life situation. Through internal channels, he found out that CitiBank was looking for just such an application for its credit-card processing operation. CitiBank wanted a better way to deal with customer inquiries, which often came in the form of letters. When CitiBank got back to a cardholder, its customer service representatives wanted to have a copy of any correspondence before them. But with cardholders writing thousands of letters to CitiBank, it became a huge undertaking to file and retrieve all that paperwork.

Through this three-way alliance, Cutaia's group designed a system for turning all those letters into electronic images—exact replicas of the originals—readily retrievable on a terminal. Through this association, we not only developed a workable system, we were able to bring significant refinements to it. For example, during development, most of our work focused on the workstations on which the images could be recalled. When the system went into actual operation at CitiBank, however, the workstations performed without a hitch. Instead, the system was so heavily used—so much paper was going into it—that it became prone to bottlenecks. We were able to break those traffic jams, but without having tested it under "shop" conditions, we probably would have introduced a troubled product to the market. Instead, we had something that really put sizzle into our new machine.

Cutaia took a similar approach for turning telephony into a real-world application. The main use we saw came from integrating the capabilities of computerized telephone switching systems—PBXs—to a commercial computer like the Silverlake. PBXs, for instance, have the capability to identify the number from which a telephone call has originated. Getting the Silverlake to work in tandem with that ability opened countless possibilities for automating common business tasks. In the case of a client calling an attorney, for example, the computer would automatically record the call and time its length for the purpose of billings. Or think of its utility to a distributor: When a customer calls in with an order, the computer automatically searches for and finds that customer's account file, displaying it onto the computer screen of the person answering the call. With the complete account history in place, the order taker transacts the calls with no delay—not for credit approvals and certainly not for looking up stock numbers of the customer's regularly purchased items.

Although we initially started a cooperative effort with IBM's Rolm subsidiary, we found that Rolm PBX's hadn't penetrated into many of the markets we had targeted. If telephony was going to be practical reality for a wide range of Silverlake users, we had to interface with PBXs made by other manufacturers. So Cutaia went out and struck alliances with other switchmakers. Then he established partnerships with five or so software vendors who had already developed applications using telephony technology, including the just described billing and order-taking programs. Once again, thanks to these alliances, we had another head-turning application we were ready to wow the marketplace with when the Silverlake made its debut.

Indeed, as we got closer to Silverlake's unveiling, more and more of the pieces it would take to make the new machine an indisputable success were falling into place. We were building an inventory of applications, including some gee-whiz advanced ones, and creating a pool of expertise to provide first-class service and support. But we couldn't have done it on our own. We had to lower the drawbridge at Fortress Rochester to let outsiders into the development process. We learned a tremendous amount from our customers and Business Partners. They told us what they considered important in a technology and how to make it useful to them. They taught us how to commercialize technology. We were able to develop processes that were short, flexible, and adaptable.

By opening ourselves up, we fostered an unquantifiable amount of goodwill and loyalty among our customers. Not only were they flattered by our willingness to listen to what they had to say, but they could see that our long-term plans were in keeping with their own. As Charlie Bell, the Director of Management Information Systems at Jefferson Smurfit and a member of one of our customer councils, expressed it at the Silverlake's market introduction, "Do you realize that 90 percent of what I suggested is now in the product? I feel like I'm part of the development team."

What was the applicability to others in what we did? Our experience highlighted the new reality of doing business. No company, no enterprise, can depend entirely on its own devices anymore. Therefore, it's imperative to form partnerships. To the extent that you can, you have to let outsiders in. These include suppliers, resellers, third-party enterprises, and, most of all, customers—in other words, all the constituencies you have a stake in. They can offer you resources. They can offer you expertise. And most of all, they—especially customers—can help you to stay abreast, even ahead, of your market.

Partnerships alone, however, aren't enough. Even with

all the help the Silverlake got from outsiders, we still had an enormous amount of work to do—work that couldn't be completed with the sweat of anyone's brow but our own. If we were to get it done, on time, we had to find a way to unleash untapped stores of energy and creativity—and that meant rethinking the whole world of work at IBM Rochester.

8

EMPOWERING PEOPLE

Lead, but don't get in the way.

— STEVE SCHWARTZ, IBM Vice-President and General Manager
Application Business Systems

We were overworked and overwrought. Internal surveys showed that our managers at IBM Rochester were racking up overtime hours to the tune of 30 to 40 percent above and beyond the 40-hour week, and it was nothing for some of them to pack seven and a half regular workdays into a week. The strain was taking a terrible personal toll. Because their lives were getting so out of kilter, their marriages, their families, and their health all suffered. We knew it had to be getting bad when we began to hear about ourselves over at the nearby Mayo Clinic: During their briefings to heart patients, doctors would talk about the causes of coronary disease, including the high stress of certain occupations like "being a manager at IBM."

Many of our managers were running out of gas. But this

is what made it a problem of utmost concern: It was the fall of 1986, and the Silverlake Project had yet to get underway. We were already being stretched to the limits of endurance, and we found ourselves faced with doing *even more* if we were going to get the Silverlake to market in 28 months. Obviously, we had to find a way to become more productive. But dishing out more responsibility and pressure would have exacted a price too precious from people who had already overpaid.

We were mulling this situation at a meeting of the Rochester Management Board that fall, just as the Silverlake Project was going into full swing. Tom Furey, our leader in the development lab, made a crucial observation. He said the pyramid at IBM Rochester "was inverted"—our managers were taking on too much themselves. They were spending far too much time fighting the daily brush fires, and their "micro-managing" was coming at the expense of dealing with broader, long-term strategic matters. While our managers were sacrificing themselves to the altar of overwork, those whom they managed—the hundreds of engineers, programmers, and others who formed the reservoir of technical skills and knowledge in the development lab—were being *underutilized.*

That had to change. Furey put it quite succinctly, "If we are going to get the Silverlake out on time, we are going to share the load." We had to push ownership, responsibility, and accountability down to the point of execution—to where the real work was being done. And that was at the most grassroots level of the lab. As we did, we had to equip with education and tools the ranks of our technical professionals who would be shouldering the extra burden. Furthermore, if we were going to make the Silverlake a standard-setting machine, we also had to tap new sources of innovation. It became clear what we had to do—we had to *empower* our work force at IBM Rochester.

Empowerment is a word that has become part of the modern lexicon. A term of New Age emanations, you can hear it spoken often from the lips these days of anyone who has anything to do with organizations, from giant corporations to neighborhood church groups. But it's also one of those lofty words that brings to mind a cumulus cloud; it captures a concept that is big, dense, and, sometimes, all-too-intangibly fluffy. Strictly speaking, "empower" means to give authority, to enable. But in the world of today's organizations it means that and more. To an enterprise like IBM Rochester it meant giving people the power to get their jobs done by providing them with the resources to do it, including authority, skills, knowledge, tools, and incentives. The idea behind empowerment is to make *everyone* in an organization an effective decision-maker, not just managers. For managers, it comes down to a simple paradox: To get power—the ability to get something done—they must give power.

While concepts such as *vision* and *leadership* are about painting the big picture and steering organizations in the general direction they need to move, empowerment comes down to the nitty-gritty of *how* to get there day to day. The reason that companies of all kinds are embracing empowerment in such a big way is that organizations and their people—and the environment in which they exist—have all changed so enormously.

For most of the past century, corporations organized themselves after the very hierarchical "command-and-control" structures of military organizations. Like officers, managers gave orders that moved down a well-defined chain. Like good foot-soldiers, non-managers were to do or die and never question why. Corporations also adhered to the tenets of "scientific management," which held that a task—a manufacturing process, for example—was best broken down into its smallest, repeatable component part. The people who performed those repetitive tasks were really nothing more than any other movable part in a vast manufacturing machine. During its time, scientific management served corporations well, helping to make America's steel mills, automakers, and other factories the mightiest industrial enterprises on earth.

But during the 1980s enormous forces of change came to fruition that were to destine "command-and-control" hierarchies and the principles of scientific management to the same scrap heap that claimed so many of America's once grand industrial plants. The conditions of doing business changed. Organizations changed. The work force itself changed.

The world sped up and competition intensified. Companies could no longer afford to have decisions move up and down a lumbering bureaucracy. Things needed to get done —yesterday. A wave of takeovers put companies on notice; to survive they had to get lean and mean. Everybody "downsized", including IBM. It all meant that the same amount of work had to be done by fewer people. Companies also came to the revelation that no one knew a job better than those who were actually doing it; no one knew assembly better than those who were on the assembly line day after day. No one knew the electronics of a component better than the engineer working on it. No one knew the forecast rationale for a new product better than the planner who developed it.

In the old command-and-control organization, information flowed along prescribed channels. Managers were gatekeepers who controlled access to who knew what. But not anymore. Thanks to computer networks, E-mail, voice mail, facsimile machines, cross-functional work teams, and task forces, everyone seems to be plugged in. Even at the lowest rungs of the corporation, people have access to information—and other people—to a degree they'd never before experienced. Clerks and secretaries have never been more well informed and, therefore, never more capable —and motivated—to act on the basis of their own sound judgment.

Indeed, those same clerks and secretaries—and the majority of those now composing the work force—grew up in an era where authority was no longer accepted without question. What's more, because they are coming to depend more on brain than brawn, companies are becoming more and more populated with what management guru Peter

Drucker describes as "the knowledge worker." They are highly educated and highly skilled. It used to be that superior knowledge was a prerequisite to moving up the management ladder. But in today's complex, high-tech world, managers can only hope to know only a fraction of what the specialists who work for them do. As a result, Drucker says companies are becoming more and more akin to a symphony orchestra. The knowledge workers are the musicians. A manager is the conductor, keeping everybody on cue but never thinking of telling the first chair how to actually play the violin.

All these same dynamics were coming into play at IBM Rochester as we embarked on the Silverlake Project. And if we didn't see these trends unfolding before our eyes, we were reading about them in *Fortune* magazine. But it wasn't these broad forces alone that provided us with the impetus to change. Our mandate emerged, too, from factors unique to our development laboratory.

The failure of Fort Knox had alerted us to the error of having managers make technical decisions that really belonged to experts in the trenches. The multiple computers-in-one approach to Fort Knox came from on high. Technical wizards like Pete Hansen and Jim Flynn from down below had sallied forth to say that trying to make Fort Knox the single replacement for IBM's already existing mid-range machines just wasn't feasible, but only succeeded in getting themselves out of the project. They were right as it turned out. So one of the object lessons to emerge from the Fort Knox experience was that managers are the rightful owners of *business* decisions, those involving the things that make a business go and grow—strategy, budgets, profitability, personnel, planning, marketing, and the like. But they shouldn't get directly and intimately entangled in the specialized details of implementation. At that level of minutiae, the specialists—in our case, the engineers and programmers of the development lab—should have the say. In retrospect, what happens with micromanagement is tantamount to the chairman of General Motors declaring, "We're going to develop a luxury car of

Japanese quality and European looks that sells for $15,000, and, oh, by the way, here's how the carburetor is going to work."

Our managers at IBM Rochester tended to be too meddling too. Our culture made them that way, because it bred an overdependence on managerial ranks. We tended to be especially reliant on our front-line managers who oversaw department-sized units of from anywhere of 10 to 20 people. This stemmed in part from an overall IBM philosophy that front-line managers are the key to the corporation's health. IBM regards its front-line managers as the guardians of the corporation's most cherished tenet—respect for the individual—and thus as the keepers of company morale. IBM considers its front-line managers its main contact with its work force, the nodes from which it can communicate its visions, policies, and upper management decisions. The corporation even has vested in its front-line managers the rather heady responsibility to hire and fire.

At IBM Rochester, we put even more on our managers. According to the mores of our culture, a department manager was expected to be on top of everything. Never mind that this entailed keeping abreast of three or more highly technical projects all at once, we demanded that our managers be very technically knowledgeable. During management meetings, they were expected to authoritatively address most technical questions relating to the units and projects they oversaw at a very detailed level. To have to rely on one of the technical experts who worked for them to explain some arcane complexity would have been seen as a major sign of weakness.

As a result, our managers found themselves under enormous pressure to have their noses in all the doings of their departments. Because of the expectations placed on them by IBM's philosophy and our own local culture, they felt compelled to micro-manage. Between trying to keep up with brain-twisting technical developments and putting out the fires of day-to-day problems, they were diverting their attentions away from the more paramount issues of getting

140

our computers to market faster and at ever higher levels of quality.

It was no wonder our managers were logging so much overtime and suffering from the strain. It didn't help their blood pressure either knowing that, in IBM, front-line management is a make-or-break opportunity. Anyone with ambitions for moving up the management ladder has to give a stand-out performance while they're on that lowermost rung. Given all this, we shouldn't have been surprised that the Mayo doctors invoked our name by way of exemplifying a high health-risk occupation.

Management wasn't our only career track, though. We actually had another. At IBM Rochester you could move up through a series of technical positions of ascending responsibility, pay, and prestige. This dual track was established to recognize the importance of individuals with a given technical talent or expertise. In this way, we were like a magazine, which has editors and writers. Editors oversee writers. But if you're a good writer with no interest or knack for dealing with other writers you can still advance to become a senior writer or even a columnist.

The problem was that, while our managers were being taken to the limits of mortal endurance, those on the technical track were clamoring for us to give them more responsibility. During the roundtable meetings he held as a prelude to articulating his vision, Furey heard time and again expressions of frustration coming from our technical rank-and-file. "We're capable of taking the ball on this matter or that one and running with it," they told him. "We're grown up, mature, educated adults, and we've spent years developing our competence. We think we can be trusted to do these things on our own, without having a manager—who knows half as much as we do—get in the way."

Hearing these complaints only reinforced Furey's own frustrations with some of the things he'd noticed about our technical staff. In the other IBM development labs where he'd worked, technical experts often appeared before the management councils. Yet, aside from his roundtables, he seldom had any direct contact with the technical professionals at IBM Rochester. Moreover, when Furey had a question he liked to go to the best and most direct source for an answer. He wanted to hear the words from *the* technical expert, not some manager who was, after all, providing secondhand information bound to have lost something in the translation.

Even more disturbing was the fact that, despite our impressive output over the years, our development lab ranked in the lower third of 15 IBM development sites on measures of "technical vitality" as tracked by corporate headquarters. We were publishing fewer technical papers than most other sites. We were applying for fewer patents. We had only one Senior Technical Staff Member, a position at the top rung of the technical hierarchy, while other sites had seven on average. We had no IBM Fellows, the distinction the company confers on technical professionals who establish a consistent track record of making world-class technical contributions to the company.

To find out why, we turned to Roy Bauer, to whom Furey had entrusted responsibility for dealing with one of our most precious resources—our people. Bauer began conducting a series of focus groups among our programmers, engineers, and other technical types. From them we learned that, if our lab seemed to languish when it came to innovation, it wasn't for any lack of ambition on their part —they simply didn't have the resources they needed. Managers had secretaries to help them write their letters, reports, and memos, for example, but if our technical people wanted to write something they had to peck it out on their own and the bureaucracy they had to go through hardly made it worthwhile. To publish a paper they had to obtain a series of approvals, sometimes all the way up to IBM headquarters. For patents they had to deal with a phalanx of lawyers and a mountain of paper. Even if they went to all this trouble, what was in it for them? Aside from seeing their name in print, there was little tangible reward.

All these problems were actually symptomatic of a work force whose talents and energies were being kept in shackles. If we were going to fulfill our vision for Silverlake and ourselves, we had to free it from those chains. In the broad sense, we knew what had to be done. First, we wanted to get our managers to *lead* more and manage less. By that we meant that managers were to set broad goals and guidelines and provide the support to help *others* get their jobs done. In short, we wanted managers to tell people where they had to go and trust them to decide how they were going to get there. Furey had already set this example for us himself when he'd so often send us away with the words, "That's not my decision to make, it's yours."

When they did manage, we wanted them not to manage people as much as they managed the process. And we wanted them to skillfully manage the risks associated with this management style. This was our way of saying that, while people should be left to their own devices to get where they had to go, it was up to our managers to make sure they remained on track and to understand the goals that needed to be achieved. Managers were to smooth the way by removing obstacles and seeing to it that people had the resources they needed. They were not, however, to abdicate complete control; instead, as they were doling out authority, they were also to be handing out accountability to make certain that people didn't wander off into the wrong direction.

At the same time we wanted managers to push authority and accountability down into the ranks, we wanted to make sure our programmers and engineers were ready to accept it. If managers were going to give them more responsibility, our technical professionals had to want to take it. At the time, we articulated all this in just three words: Enable, excite, and reward. But we just as well could have said it in one: Empower.

We also knew that this was all easier said than done. It's one thing to *tell* managers they have to delegate and quite another to get them to do it. It's one thing to *tell*

143

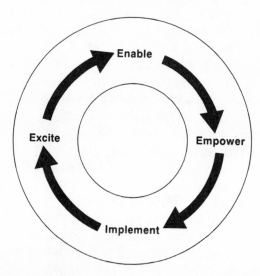

Figure 10. Empowerment strategy

people they need to take on more responsibility and quite another to get them to accept it. It was going to involve more than cheerleading on our part. So Bauer instituted several very tangible, very specific measures to take empowerment from lofty ideal to reality.

Managers had to share the load. In what may be hardest thing for managers to do, they had to give up some of their authority to others. Those they managed would take on this extra degree of responsibility and authority. To accomplish all that, one of the first things we did was to spell out, very specifically, what we *expected*—what we expected managers to give in terms of responsibilities and what we expected their people to do in terms of taking it. We did this through our performance planning, counseling, and appraisal system. At least once a year, all our employees are evaluated on a range from excellent to unsatisfactory. But the expectations to which people were supposed to perform weren't explicitly spelled out, or were inconsistently applied. What happened all too often was that a manager in one department had a different standard than a manager in another.

What Bauer did was to form a *cross-functional* work team consisting of people representing the various functions within the lab. For each and every position in the lab—programmers, engineers, microcoders, market planners, business planners, managers, etc.—this team elaborated on what a lab employee had to do, specifically, to reach each one of four rating levels on the evaluation scale. In many cases, these included more than 50 criteria grouped into seven areas—quality, productivity, planning, technical competence, leadership, relationships, and communications. For example, for senior engineers in product development to earn an excellent rating, they had to deliver high-risk work with high quality, carry an unusually heavy work load, maintain the highest performance during a crisis, generate one patent a year, publish something in a professional journal, and influence group morale positively.

We compiled all these guidelines into a thick three-ring binder for managers. We called the managers together in the cafeteria and explained to them its purpose. In creating this handbook, we brought more objectivity and, therefore, fairness to the appraisal process, which was especially important now that we were going to ask everyone to be doing so much more to get Silverlake out the door. Someone who worked their tail off for an "excellent" rating didn't have to worry about a colleague in a similar job breezing their way to the very same rating just because their manager happened to be more laid back.

Although this may have seemed bureaucratic and restrictive, it was, in fact, liberating. Empowerment shouldn't be confused with total freedom, or the corporate equivalent of anarchy. Everyone has to have boundaries and standards, and it can be empowering just to let people know what boundaries and standards they're expected to meet. Guessing at that is one of the biggest banes of corporate existence. So people in organizations often yearn to know exactly *what* is expected of them. What becomes disempowering is when they're told *how* they're supposed to meet expectations and detailed objectives—that's when they become subject to managerial meddling.

By giving managers these guidelines, we also provided them with an important tool, one that did a few other things too. It outlined the kinds of responsibilities managers could shift from themselves to those who worked for them. Most of all, the handbook "raised the bar of expectations" for our non-management staff. It not only delineated what responsibilities they were to take on, but, in one stroke, it concretely established the standards to which everyone would have to rise for us to fulfill the lofty vision we had set for ourselves.

Indeed, providing people with the tools—the means—of empowerment is absolutely crucial. Thanks to modern training regimens, today's Olympic-class pole vaulters may be stronger and more well conditioned than anyone who's ever taken on the event. But no matter how strong and well conditioned, no matter how hard they work at it, they couldn't soar to heights of 20 feet or more if they still used wooden poles instead of lightweight, flexible ones made of space-age materials. You can't expect people in an organization to achieve new heights just by working harder. If you do, they'll just become cynical. That's why so many managers and organizations fail at their efforts to empower. They talk about how they want people to vault, but that's all it is—talk, or a corporate form of cheerleading. Metaphorically speaking, they fail to supply their people with poles made of space-age materials.

But at IBM Rochester, we did. Bauer launched several initiatives to *enable* the people of the development lab. He saw to it they were equipped with skills, techniques, and tools. And he did it for people in both management and technical ranks.

We took a number of steps to nurture a new generation of managers who were also leaders. We appointed a person to work full time on management development issues. Through this position, we set forth a specific set of criteria for what it took to become a manager. We established 22 different requirements. Anyone who aspired to management had to have cross-functional experience, so we could be assured they could deal with broad issues. They had to have some recent continuing education. They had to have completed a leadership course we offered on site. They had to have exposure to customers and marketing. They had to work on high-impact projects that required risk taking. They had to have leadership assignments such as chairing a task force, or a cross-functional team that gave them visibility and tested their judgment.

To enforce these standards we made it mandatory for all candidates for promotion to be screened by our management development specialist. No proposed promotion could be approved without his seeing it first. Although his role in such matters was always advisory, his review powers helped enforce our standards. The screening served to put the managers who were making the recommendations for promotion on notice: If they wanted their people to climb the ladder, they had to have a hand in developing them along the lines we'd set forth.

To encourage people to make the right decisions about whether they even wanted to be managers, we began holding a monthly series of luncheon briefings, called Management Preparation seminars. At each session, a front-line manager would appear before the group to talk about what the job entailed, its rewards and its frustrations. This turned out to be a particularly good self-screening measure. We often plucked our managers from the ranks of programmers, engineers, and other technical types. But, in many cases, those who made the switch found they didn't really savor a manager's main task of dealing with other people. They really preferred the challenge of wrestling with technical issues, which meant that they tended to be interfering bosses. After raising this issue in the minds of our management aspirants, more than a few decided to happily forego a management career in favor of remaining on the technical track.

In fact, we took several steps to make it easier for them to remain on that track, mainly by making a technical career more attractive. Indeed, our technical professionals became the focus of our most significant efforts at empowerment. If the Silverlake Project was to succeed, if IBM Rochester was to become one of IBM's flagship operations, it would hinge on them. We empowered our cadres of technical pros by giving them responsibility, authority, and accountability all at once. And we did that by giving them *ownership*.

The hardware and software shops in our development lab comprised some 175 department-sized groups, each one responsible for some specific component of the Silverlake Project. This was no different from other computer development projects we'd undertaken. But before Silverlake, all the thousands of specifications for performance, cost, and quality, plus the schedule for getting the work done, came down from the top. For the Silverlake Project, however, only very broad system specifications were set from on high. We actually left it to programmers and engineers in each of the working departments to determine their own detailed objectives for performance, cost, quality, and completion date. All they had to do was stay within the broad guidelines. In this way, each component of Silverlake actually became their own.

By taking this tack, we also encouraged a fairly high degree of communication and cross-pollination between individual departments. In many cases, if a group wanted to meet the specs they'd set for themselves, they'd have to negotiate tradeoffs. For example, some programmers might have established for themselves creating a certain function at a certain cost and performance criteria. When they got down to it, though, they may have discovered they'd committed themselves to the impossible. The only way they could make good on that commitment would be to get some engineering modifications. So off they would go—to the appropriate group of hardware engineers to hammer out a design change that would permit them to meet their programming specs.

What this meant was that our technical people were becoming self-managed—precisely what we wanted. As the work on Silverlake raced along, millions of decisions had to be made. We didn't have time to wait for them to go up the hierarchy and come back down to be resolved. Because we'd vested ownership—and authority—at the very grassroots levels of our lab, many of these day-to-day issues were often resolved on the spot. The owners of a component came to grips with it among themselves, or in cross-functional teams. By giving people ownership—and the freedom to use their initiative—some amazing things began to happen. We began to see some extraordinary examples of empowerment at work.

Take the case of our smallest Silverlake. As it was originally conceived, the Silverlake line was to consist of four models, each one bigger than the next. But after work on the Silverlake Project was underway, our market analysis indicated that we needed to add to the bottom end another, even smaller model. Futhermore, the decision we'd reached in the Rochester Management Board to make a small version of the System/36 turned out to be so successful with customers that they insisted we had to offer something similar as part of the Silverlake line. To take on this effort, we turned to Duane Dueker, a hardware engineer who'd just returned to Rochester after an assignment in Japan. Furey essentially told Dueker, "We want a low-end model; go to it."

And that was it. Dueker started from scratch. He had no design, no people, no funding, nothing. Even worse, we were giving Dueker a late start. We wanted him to have his small model ready with the rest of the line, which meant he had *less than two years to complete his part of the project.* Dueker went off and formed a team. But when they went to work, they faced several extraordinary challenges.

The first involved design. Everything about the Silverlake's original design had been predicated on a four-model line. Everything was done to optimize the functions, features, cost, and price of those four original models. But we were asking Dueker and his group do something never intended in the original design. It was as though we were asking him to take the blueprints and parts for a Cadillac and turn them into a GEO Storm. But Dueker and his group did just that. They came up with some innovative packaging ideas and ways to adapt parts and components from Silverlake's bigger models into use for their low-end model.

Their second challenge concerned price. Small computers are particularly price-sensitive products. The reason is simple: The customers buying small computers are usually small businesses, which really have to watch a dollar. If you price a small computer too high it will give competition an advantage. And in that business there are plenty of aggressive competitors. So the tricky part of creating a small computer is finding just the right mix of features and functions that will allow you to offer a competitive machine—at a competitive price. To determine what that mix of features and functions should be, Bruce Anthony, an engineer, and Johnie Wooten, one of our planners, took it upon themselves to do a study using conjoint analysis, which provided the basis for giving the machine the proper price-performance balance. It was not only remarkable that these two did the study on their own but that they introduced a new cross-functional collaborative methodology between engineering and planning. They simply broke new ground.

The most remarkable thing, however, was that Dueker's group had the small model ready for introduction with the rest of the line. They created their own computer in less than 24 months. But they would never have been able to accomplish this feat without the almost entrepreneurial degree of ownership, authority, and freedom that they were given in tackling their part of the Silverlake Project.

In another notable case, a group of engineers were convinced that they could get some chips they'd designed to run faster. They believed they could improve the speed not by changing the design but by altering the way the chips were being made at our East Fishkill, New York, chip-manufacturing facility. (Because chips are so intricate, the manufacturing process plays a big role in their ultimate performance.) The IBM Rochester engineers broached their idea to the engineers at East Fishkill, who reacted by saying it couldn't be done. Our engineers wouldn't take "no" for an answer.

They returned to Rochester where we have a small prototype chip-manufacturing line, one capable of making chips in small, experimental lots. Using the line, they proved that their suggested way of changing the manufacturing process was indeed doable. They went back to East Fishkill where the engineers, faced with tangible results of workability, had no choice but to implement the manufacturing changes. And we not only got faster chips, we managed to lower the per-chip cost too. Even better, the faster, cheaper chips allowed us to add a more powerful model to the upper end of the Silverlake line. So shortly after Silverlake came to market, this new seventh model was introduced as our highest performance machine. Thanks to our efforts at empowerment, we created a broader line with a wider appeal to more kinds of customers.

Of course, ownership and authority didn't come without accountability. Schleicher held his programmer's feet to the fire. For example, they had to weigh in daily with progress and quality reports, which we carefully tracked over time; at the first sign of any serious deviation from either our timetable or our quality standards we were ready to call in the "Bug Stompers," our troubleshooting team of programmers. To make sure our component level decisions didn't mount up to the point of threatening the integrity of our basic design for the machine, all changes had to be reported to watchdog bodies called Design Control Groups (DCG). There were six DCGs in all, each consisting of three to four programming experts who would intercede when a decision infringed on the viability of some other part of the system or breached the integrity of our high-level specifications for the Silverlake. The DCGs also saved time by keeping design-change decision making close to where the work was being done. Approvals simply didn't have to climb through a big bureaucracy.

To help our technical people make the Silverlake a cutting-edge machine, we had to nurture innovation among

151

them. We did that and simultaneously reinvigorated our reputation for technical vitality. We hired consultants who held a series of two-day "innovation workshops" in which they lectured and took our technical professionals through a series of exercises to help them break the bonds of their routine ways of thinking. We did re-educating of a weightier kind too. To get our planners to think more in terms of markets and less in products, for example, we held quarterly seminars taught by some of the finest minds in academia. These included marketing gurus Philip Kotler of the Kellogg School at Northwestern University and Jerry Wind of the Wharton School at the University of Pennsylvania, management theorist Noel Tichy of the University of Michigan, and strategies consultant Ram Charan. In so doing, we equipped our planners with world-class skills, tools, and techniques. We made huge strides in transforming them from a group of generic planners into a world-class group of product, market, and business planners.

Not all of our education was so formalized. The technology embodied in the Silverlake was similar to that of its System/38 predecessor. But the majority of our programmers and engineers had been assigned to the System/36, which was far different. The System/36 people accounted for a big part of the development lab's pool of personnel. We also needed to bring a great deal of System/36 capabilities to Silverlake. We simply didn't have the time, however, to get these System/36 people up to snuff on the Silverlake architecture by putting them through chalkboard instruction. So we exposed people from each group to on-the-job training through a process of "cross-pollination." We carefully mixed System/36 and System/38 people together in component-level teams. People learned from each other.

To stimulate invention, Bauer pressed to make it less of a hassle for our technical professionals to apply for patents. We gathered our patent attorneys together to streamline the patent application process. They suggested turning a large part of the patent review and recommendation process over to line managers rather than the legal department. Once these changes were made, it took only four to six months to get a patent filed instead of 12 months. To get our technical professionals to share their ideas—and to help them gain recognition—we instituted a new incentives program. For publishing an internal technical memo they received one point, for a book they got 10 points. Once they accumulated 12 points they earned a $1,200 bonus. The higher the point total, the bigger the bonus.

It's said that workers are only as good as their tools, and we made every effort to see that our people—technical professionals and managers alike—were given the implements they needed. Those tools included the multimillion dollar Engineering Verification Engine, or EVE, the computer that allowed us to actually test our designs through system simulation, as well as powerful high-function computer workstations that gave programmers more capability. Emilio Collar and his troops compiled their volumes of market and competitive analysis into an on-line database accessible not only to our planners but to managers at IBM Rochester. Through it, our managers had at their fingertips up-to-date information, often in graphic form, on our financial performance, productivity, market share, and industry and competitive trends. Collar made sure the system was easy and intuitive for everyone to use. Suddenly, planners and managers could call on a panoply of data that provided them with a big picture, helping to elevate their thinking from narrow day-to-day concerns to broader strategic ones. By offering them up-to-the-minute data for analysis, managers were able to make more informed decisions—and faster. It has been said that "people without information cannot take responsibility, but people who are given information cannot help but take responsibility." And so it was.

Since our long-term goal was to transform IBM Rochester into a *market-driven* enterprise, we had to condition everyone to give primacy to customer concerns. To foster a greater sensitivity to customers, we participated in several programs championed by Site General Manager Larry Osterwise. Top executives and technical professionals were assigned to key customers whom they went out into the field to visit about once every six weeks. Under another

153

Osterwise initiative, programmers, engineers, and manufacturing people did six-week stints on temporary assignment in sales. We also had a program through which anyone at IBM Rochester could volunteer for a six-month to a one-year assignment doing telephone surveys among customers. When we held our customer councils, we televised the proceedings into conference rooms where anyone could come to hear and see what our customers had to say about Silverlake. Finally, Schleicher's Software Partners Laboratory gave engineers and programmers a day-to-day opportunity to interact with customers.

Another key to empowerment is communication. If we were going to give our hands, our heads, and, most of all, our hearts, we were the kind of educated work force that demanded to know the what and why behind our mission, and where we stood. Furey made sure we were fully informed. Along with his continuing series of roundtables, we began publishing a monthly newsletter entitled "Lab Director's Report." We hired a full-time communications employee. Furey also continued to hold all-manager and all-employee meetings. They were often so elaborate and well done that people began to joke that Furey had missed his real calling—as a Hollywood producer.

But we needed someone to communicate the full impact of the value of Silverlake. We found her in Julie Furey, manager of the Rochester Executive Briefing Center, which reported to IBM U.S. sales. She built a brand-new briefing center she called "Solutions Showcase", and her staff developed a set of comprehensive demonstrations that were so forceful and compelling they became a "must" for IBM executives, customers, and Business Partners.

Our processes to empower—to enable, excite, and reward —worked. We provided those who worked at IBM Rochester with the resources to get the job done, including authority, skills, knowledge, tools, and incentives. We made *everyone* an effective decision-maker, not just managers. By giving power, we got power.

Even though our work became more intense and the pressure mounted, morale actually began to rise. Our own formal internal surveys clearly tracked the ascent. People worked harder than ever before—not because they had to but because they wanted to. In one instance, one of our programmers accepted a promotion that took him off the project, but he did it only on one condition. He insisted that the company buy him a computer so he could continue to work on his part of the Silverlake—at home during the evenings!

On almost every measure of technical vitality our performance vaulted. The technical publications started pouring out of IBM Rochester. In a single year while Silverlake was still in development, technical memos (for internal consumption only) jumped 138 percent; internal presentations that eventually made for published proceedings went up by 32 percent. Eventually, patent applications climbed too, rising 82 percent. We added Al Cutaia to our ranks of IBM Fellow, and increased the number of Senior Technical Staff Members in our lab from one to five. Before long we became known as *the* hotbed of technical innovation within IBM. Not only did other parts of IBM ask us to talk to them about our technical achievements and the whole issue of innovation, we actually started to get invitations from *other companies*.

But the biggest indication of our success was our schedule. The work was getting done and on time. By early 1988, we knew we had made it. We were going to complete the Silverlake, a standard-setting machine, in the unheard-of time frame of 28 months. We were going to hit our window of opportunity. Even the highest councils of IBM thought we couldn't do it, but the Silverlake was headed for its debut by the summer of 1988.

If there was a lesson in this accomplishment, it was that empowerment can be an extraordinary force in organizations. Empowerment is the process of putting power into the hands of people at the most grassroots level of an organization. It's a matter of providing them with the authority, the freedom, and the trust to use their talents and energies. But people aren't empowered as if by magic. It takes more than saying, "I empower you." You have to back them up with resources—by giving them tools, techniques, and skills. Not surprisingly, many managers will not give up their authority readily. You have to help them over the hump, as we did, by defining precisely what responsibilities you want them to share. Finally, empowerment isn't to be mistaken as a laissez-faire approach to management. Along with giving people authority, organizations also must build in ways to hold people accountable.

We did all these things. And, to our surprise, we got more work done than ever. The Silverlake was right on track for its debut. So by mid-1987, almost a year before its planned unveiling, we began to prepare for Silverlake's formal introduction. During its development, the Silverlake Project had become one of IBM's worst-kept secrets. Of course, we'd never been so open about a project before. Almost from the time of its inception, our industry had been abuzz with rumors and speculation about the new machine. With its appetite whet by all the anticipation, the market developed a set of expectations that were intimidatingly high. So we knew: It was going to take more than giving the market an excellent machine, we had to *present* it just so. Silverlake's launch had to be extra-special. If its introduction fell short, we risked causing a disappointment in the market that could mortally wound our beloved machine—and render all our work for naught.

9

REINVENTING THE LAUNCH

This world-wide launch looks impossible.

—RALPH F. CLARK, Manager of Strategic Planning, IBM Rochester

It began even before the Silverlake left the drawing boards. After Fort Knox, our customers and Business Partners couldn't help wondering what we were going to do. Then we declared the System/38 "non-strategic"—IBM-speak for the decision to eventually discontinue the line. Advancements to the System/36 started slowing down, indicating that its days were numbered too.

The entire mid-range market was in turmoil. A growing number of competitors were joining the fracas into which the mid-range had turned. At the very same time, there were predictions that the mid-range computer would go the way of the dodo, squeezed into extinction by the shrinkage in size and price of mainframes and the explosion in the power and popularity of personal computers. Questions began to mount. Was IBM committed to the mid-range sector? Was it about to retire from the mid-range altogether? Was it conceding the mid-range market to the competition?

Then hints began to emerge. We were up to something. Steve Schwartz, the head of IBM's mid-range business, started telling our customers that IBM's mid-range strategy had two pillars, of which Rochester systems was one. Was a machine on the way? The project's code name leaked. Silverlake? The trade press picked up on the handle. What would it be like? How powerful? What features? Customers had poured billions of dollars into buying our systems. Would they have to eat the investment because we'd made their old computers obsolete—like a car without parts or anyone to repair it anymore? Many of our Business Partners, the independent resellers and software developers with ties to us, had cast their fates with us too. What would happen to their life's work? With some urgency one said, "Look, I've just taken a second mortgage to get the money for my business." He implored, "You've got to tell me what you're going to do in this market."

By early 1988, as we approached the Silverlake's official debut, the nearly two years of speculation that had surrounded the project built to a crescendo. Gossip and conjecture swirled around us everywhere. The scuttlebutt was that we were doing something big, very big. The trade press started giving us more and more coverage. It got to the point where some of it had the smack of tabloid sensationalism.

We took it all in with amazement—and amusement. But then the trade press starting touting us as the next "VAX killer." We began to sweat it; suddenly, we realized the dangerous heights to which expectations for the Silverlake had ascended.

VAX was the name belonging to the line of mid-range computers made by Digital Equipment Company. As some saw it, DEC was so competitive we had to counter. Everyone was so eager to see our response that, in 1986, when IBM introduced a new mid-range computer the trade press immediately acclaimed it as the company's long-awaited frontal assault against DEC. Our machine was called the IBM 9370. But in the headlines it became known as the "VAX killer."

Never mind that it was never intended to be that. The IBM 9370 was originally conceived as one of two families —the other being the Silverlake—that would replace IBM's five disparate mid-range lines. It was aimed at offering the owners of IBM's popular System/370 mainframe computers —mostly Fortune 500-sized companies—a way to bring 370-compatible capabilities to departments or branch offices in a smaller, more affordable box. Nevertheless, IBM started believing its own press clippings. We were lulled into a false sense of security. What a mistake.

By all accounts, the IBM 9370 was a technological standout. Its problems had little to do with the machine itself. Instead, the better part of its misfortunes stemmed from the fact that the press and other outsiders took the lead to *position* the IBM 9370 in the market. Speculation, not planning, played the bigger role in establishing how it was perceived in the minds of customers. And that speculation, gossip really, raised expectations and assigned to the 9370 certain attributes it didn't have, nor was it ever intended to have. If there was something to blame, it's that we did little to set the market straight.

We learned from this experience, so when the press began attaching tags to us, we really began to worry. By so doing, the press and outsiders were positioning us in markets where we had absolutely no intention of competing. To apply false labels and wrong attributes we didn't even plan would have spelled a for-certain setback for the Silverlake.

Thankfully, however, we had the 9370 object lesson that proved two things. First, it showed what would happen to the Silverlake if it failed to live up to the market's similarly exalted expectations. Second, it confirmed how vital it would be to send it into the market with sustained momentum. Steve Schwartz didn't want us to learn this lesson again with the Silverlake. To make sure that we didn't, he concluded that we had to give it a proper product *launch.*

Indeed, the launch is of paramount importance to any product. In today's complex world, it's simply not enough to put a product—any product—into the marketplace to succeed on the strength of its inherent virtues. Too many inertial forces will come to bear. It may have to strain against its own obscurity or the staying power of an entrenched competitor. At the very least, it will be challenging the ever-growing flocks of new products clawing for space—one tiny, precious niche of recognition—in the end user's already overwhelmed mind.

In fact, that's what the launch is really all about—occupying mind space. Even more, it's about *retaining* that space. Thus, the launch is not to be equated with the product *announcement*, the single event that traditionally culminates the product development process. The right kind of launch involves more, much more, than holding a press conference and releasing a few bundles of balloons into the air. Instead, the launch should be seen as a *process.* It begins long before the day of debut. More important, it continues long after, perhaps for as long as the product exists. For a market-driven company, the launch marks a phase —one as important as the product development cycle itself—through which it can shape, if not control, all the factors that impinge on a product's ultimate success. And from its post-launch efforts, it can learn from the market to continuously improve the product and, therefore, prolong the conditions for success.

This revelation, however, didn't come to us until we took on the Silverlake Project. The way we normally handled the launch was not to begin preparations until the development process was three-quarters of the way completed. We brought in sales, usually at the headquarters level, and said, in effect, "Here's this wonderful machine, everyone will love it so much it's going to sell itself." Sales would scramble to get ready. We wouldn't let our sales force or our field support and service engineers in on the process until late in the cycle before the machine's coming out. Our Business Partners wouldn't be told anything until the day of announcement. On that day, we'd talk about our machine to the assembled press and customers in the glowing terms of a technical dialect that many had to decipher and interpret later. A few months after, we'd introduce the machine for shipment to foreign markets.

As we had learned from previous experiences, this approach was tantamount to tossing the machine into the choppy waters of the marketplace with cinder blocks strapped to its feet. Sales never had quite enough time to prepare. Even if announcement day came off without a glitch, our sales force wasn't ready to start selling, and our field engineers weren't able to start supporting and servicing. Even if they were, customers didn't have any applications to run on it. And, except for the few sophisticated enough to talk our "technologese," customers responded with a single question, "So what is this machine going to *do* for me?" And by introducing the machine in a way that made it appear as an afterthought to foreign markets, we were saying to our foreign customers, "You're just not that important."

For a long time we were lucky to be successful despite ourselves. Before we went on the defensive in the mid-range market, we could launch a machine like this and get away with it. But now we were back on our heels. Given our situation, we couldn't take any chances. When Silverlake went into the marketplace we had to be sure—absolutely certain —that we gave it every possible edge.

Silverlake's launch was to be of unprecedented proportions. We had already decided that Silverlake had to be introduced to the *world*. After all, 60 percent of System/36 and System/38 sales came from abroad. So right from conception the Silverlake was meant to be a global product. But we also needed to make a statement. We wanted to say to the market: We're in the mid-range market to stay, and in a big, big way. And we wanted to send a message to our foreign customers: You're as important to us as any other customer segment.

The significance of this launch was signaled from the

very top. John Akers, our chairman, was fully aware that on Silverlake the company was staking its fortunes in the mid-range market. IBM had to have a presence, and a strong one, there. If it didn't, it couldn't fulfill its strategy of providing top-to-bottom offerings—mainframes all the way down to personal computers. So important did Akers consider this launch that in mid-1987—halfway through Silverlake's development—he personally appointed a key executive in charge of it.

The executive was William Grabe, a lithe, blond, marathon runner who had made his way up through the sales and marketing ranks to eventually head the division that handled IBM's large national accounts in the U.S. market. Grabe was also a key executive in a major product group, which meant that, along with sales, he also understood the nuances of product development. Grabe was known for his organizational acumen; decisive and deliberate, he got things done with style and finesse. Grabe was also well connected, especially within the sales ranks. He carried the confidence of IBM's executive ranks. Most of all, however, he had the chairman's imprimatur to wield. He formally reported to Steve Schwartz, but Grabe was also at the end of a dotted line that went right into Akers' office. Grabe, in short, had clout.

We'd never started preparing for a launch so soon in the development process. But Grabe wasted no time getting down to work. As one of his first acts, he started *putting the right people in the right places*. More precisely, he created an organization to carry out the work involved in the launch. He formed a *cross-functional team* called the Executive Steering Committee. Co-chaired by Grabe and Schwartz, the Executive Steering Committee consisted of representatives from all the functions involved in Silverlake, including the development lab, manufacturing, finance, marketing, and sales. Tom Furey was a member, as were the top sales executives from each one of IBM's five geographically based groups—the United States, Europe, Canada, Asia-Pacific, and Latin America. In its makeup and mission, the Executive Steering Committee was similar to

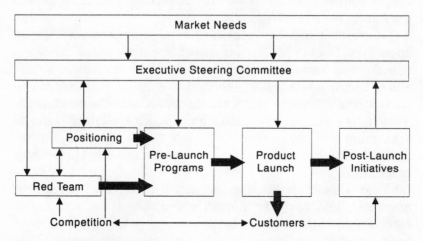

Figure 11. Launch process

the Project Management Team headed by our own Jim Coraza, Silverlake's system manager. Both were aimed at coordinating the efforts of the far-flung parts of IBM with roles in the Silverlake Project. But while Coraza's group focused on the operational end of the project—development and manufacturing—the Executive Steering Committee concentrated on marketing, sales readiness, and post-launch initiatives.

To gear up for the sales and marketing effort, Grabe and the Executive Steering Committee relied heavily on the market *segmenting, targeting, and positioning* work we had done.

In the past, the sales programs for a new machine were so generalized as to be generic. To give them the broadest possible applicability, we geared them to a customer representing some ephemeral average. No real customer, or market, ever resembled this mythical average. Take banking. In aggregate, the banking institutions that appeared to be our best prospects were the biggest. But when we got down to specifics through our segmenting analysis, we actually found that, as a group, small community banks in the rural heartland represented a much

163

bigger source of demand for the Silverlake line than all the big banks together.

To oversee this key part of the sales preparation, Grabe appointed Debbie Miller, an unequivocating sales executive who'd once served as assistant to IBM chairman Frank Cary. Under her auspices, she led a comprehensive effort so that virtually every sales territory around the globe conducted its own segmentation analysis. This allowed them to determine the best way to reach these markets, either through our own sales force or our associated third-party resellers.

With this in hand they targeted their most promising markets, right down to a level where they could *create and execute customized sales programs to reach customers in their territory*. In contrast to many sales programs of the past that were generic, these were specific and could be put into action.

Debbie Miller was able to carry forward in a similarly concrete way with the positioning we had articulated. To differentiate it from its competitors, we had decided to position the Silverlake in terms of its benefits—a business could grow with it, it embodied a solution to a business task or problem, it was simple to use, it would enhance productivity, and it was backed by support and service. Tang and Collar working with Northwestern University marketing professor Phil Kotler's consulting help took this a step forward to come up with a positioning approach that captured the essence of the Silverlake—and the strategy behind it.

It was similar to the positioning strategy embodied in the way students of marketing describe Ford Motor Company's enormously successful Taurus: "The family car, with Japanese quality, European styling, at an American price." We thought our message was just as succinctly apropos: "Silverlake, the easy-to-use and productive application business system for growing businesses." This statement formed the basis for articulating not only our overall sales and marketing approach but all our supporting collateral, advertising, and public relations.

164

In the intensely competitive environment that character-ized the mid-range market, we knew that, once Silverlake hit the market, our rivals would be opening up on it with all the firepower they had. We wanted to be ready for their counter-attacks. To get us in trim, Grabe borrowed an idea from the military. The U.S. Air Force has what it calls an "aggressor squadron" trained in the tactics of enemy fighter pilots. As a way to prepare for an actual air battle, pilots go against the members of the aggressor squadron in simu-lated dogfights. Grabe formed our own aggressor squadron. We called it the Red Team, and it consisted of 20 people, all of them battle-hardened veterans handpicked from the trenches of sales. For three months, the Red Team studied and dissected the Silverlake and its sales strategy just as a competitor would.

They pointed out actual weaknesses. For example, they told us that the Silverlake would be placed under a micro-scope to determine its capability to communicate with com-petitive machines, a problem that we immediately ad-dressed by enhancing features and functions in that key area. The Red Team also warned us to stay focused and avoid potentially errant efforts, recommending, for instance, that the Silverlake avoid nonbusiness markets, such as the one for scientific applications. Finally, they came up with what our competitors would try to construe as weaknesses. But with the Red Team's report in hand, we were able to prepare, well ahead of time, our rebuttals not only to the competition but to the trade press or just about any other detractor.

Above all else, we wanted to make sure that Silverlake worked as we said it would—and under a variety of dif-ferent circumstances. Nothing would damage the Silver-lake's credibility more than if it failed to deliver on our promises. This meant we had to set the right expectations in the customer's mind, the trade press, and industry con-sultants. We were able to certify Silverlake's performance capabilities through the Migration Invitational, which put hundreds of customers and Business Partners behind the keyboard. But that wasn't enough.

Thanks to our fast-track development process that helped us *break time barriers*, manufacturing ramped up for production early—so early that it was producing machines en masse well ahead of announcement day. With machines coming off the assembly lines, we began sending them out to customers and Business Partners, so they could put the Silverlake through its paces under "live" conditions. Through this early-ship program we placed 4,755 machines with customers and Business Partners of all kinds, everywhere. Many of the same customers who'd served on our councils received machines. For example, we sent a machine all the way to a customer in Bangkok, Thailand.

Under our deal with them, these customers were to use these machines on the side, so to speak—on a test basis only. We didn't want them to turn off their old computers. If something went wrong, we didn't want to bring someone's business to a halt before we knew we were ready. But some customers got so excited, they couldn't wait. Builder's Square, for example, a building and lumber chain, actually switched over to the Silverlake the week before Memorial Day—one of its biggest and busiest periods. The Silverlake worked without a hitch. In fact, throughout this six-month early-ship verification process, we encountered no major problems, a testament to our emphasis on *getting it right the first time*.

Of course, with a new machine—any new machine—customers were bound to have questions. When they did, the recipients of these early-ship machines could call a "Help Desk." We manned the "Help Desk" by bringing in field support and service engineers to do short stints on the phones. So not only were we there with assistance, reinforcing our commitment of support even before the machine went to market, but we also created yet another occasion to train our support people on the Silverlake well ahead of its introduction. This augmented the training our field engineers had received during the Migration Invitational. But to make absolutely certain our systems engineers, all of them, were ready we put the entire field support and service staff through a three-day training seminar.

166

During this pre-launch phase of the process, Grabe and his group also addressed the crucial issue of "packaging an offering." This was a concern that went far beyond the box in which the Silverlake would arrive at the customer's door. We used "packaging" in its broadest sense to mean the way that all the elements of the Silverlake—hardware, software, printers, data storage devices, even financing—came together for the customer. In the past, customers literally received our computer systems in piece-parts. The computer came in one box from one of our factories, the printer in a different one from somewhere else, and so on. After they unpacked and hooked it all up, customers had to load the software and then jigger with it some too. If they wanted to lease the computer from us, they had to follow one trail of paperwork. If they wanted to license the software from us, they had to pursue another. If they wanted long-term service and support, they had to deal with yet a third.

In the course of *forming partnerships with our customers and other outsiders* during the development process, we found out one thing—they hated this piece-parts approach. Smaller customers especially had neither the time, the expertise, nor the inclination to be tinkering with a computer. They wanted it to operate like a television: You plug it in, you turn it on, and it works. So in response, IBM Rochester Site General Manager Larry Osterwise came up with a concept called the Total System Package. The computer went to the customer ready to go. We loaded the software onto the computer at the factory. Printers, storage devices, and other peripherals came installed or in the same box and ready to be hooked up with a simple connector. Under the Total Systems Lease, customers had to deal with one piece of paper to lease hardware or software or to contract for service and support. They had one bill to handle in paying for all three.

Packaging raised a related issue, and we dealt with that well ahead of time too. There were going to be six different models of the Silverlake, ranging in price from $15,000 to $1 million. But within this range there were thousands of different options a customer could choose from. Their selections involved things such as memory size, peripheral devices, software, financing, and support. Taking into account all these variables, the Silverlake could be sold in millions of permutations. Not all the possible configurations were legitimate; only a small percentage were. Given this, the ordering process could have been a nightmare. It was crucial for us to make sure our sales representatives were putting all the right options together.

We solved this dilemma by relying on "artificial intelligence." This is a software technology so sophisticated that it actually gives the computer the capacity to make judgments in the way that an expert engineer, for example, would. We used AI, as it's called, to create an electronic ordering system, which would judge every option in relation to every other option to make certain they would come together into a viable system. The system then would spirit the order along to our factories where a particular Silverlake would be assembled to the exact specifications of its buyer.

Our experience with the IBM 9370 underscored the impact that image and opinion-makers—the press, consultants, market analysts—could have on the fortunes of a new machine. The way they influenced perceptions among customers could make or break the Silverlake. For past product announcements, we usually held briefings for the press and consultants, but they were generally on the day of the product unveiling. Under these conditions, the image and opinion-makers were often forced to come to snap judgments. Reporters had to rush off to make deadlines. With everything else that was going on surrounding an announcement, consultants seldom got all the information they needed from us to form considered opinions.

To make sure that the press portrayed Silverlake accurately and consultants came to informed opinions, we took a chance. After much internal debate over whether we should risk preempting our own well-planned announcement, we decided to hold an exhaustive two-day briefing for a group of the most influential reporters, columnists, and consultants who would be following the Silverlake. And we did it before the Silverlake's formal unveiling. They agreed to embargo the information until announcement day, and we agreed to tell them everything about the machine and answer any and all of their questions.

All of our top executives involved in the project—Steve Schwartz, Tom Furey, Jim Coraza, Dave Schleicher, Jim Flynn, Vic Tang, and others—made presentations. In case anyone had trouble understanding the arcane technical information we were disclosing, we put one of our engineers "on call" to translate our jargon into everyday terms. The engineer, Bruce Jawer, was just perfect for the job. Sporting a beard, tweed jacket, and glasses, he looked like central casting's pick for the part of engineer. He had a knack for putting the most complex matter into a layperson's language. No question was too technical. As someone remarked, "If Bruce didn't know the answer to a question, the question was probably invalid." We stuck a button on him that said, "Ask Bruce." By the end of the briefing he had become one of the most sought-after sources of the gathering.

Our pre-launch preparations called for us to take care of one other extraordinarily important detail—the official name for our new computer. Professor Philip Kotler from Northwestern University and many of us pressed to use the name we had known it by for so long—the Silverlake. There was something about the name that captured our fancy. The press had grabbed on to it, and because of all the pre-launch publicity we had gotten, the machine was already widely known by its code name. Why not cash in on established recognition? It was decided, however, that the name would have been too inconsistent with the nomenclature IBM applied to its computer systems company wide. So the search started for a new name.

We heard the "IBM System/9380" was in the running, but many of us considered that idea too close to the IBM 9370. Another possibility was the "System/37", a name connoting the Silverlake as a cross "in between" the System/36 and System/38. How about the System/39, as in one beyond the two existing machines?

In the end, IBM opted for the "AS/400." As we saw it, the "AS" made for a double entendre. From the beginning, we refused to see the Silverlake as just another computer. It was really a vehicle for providing our customers with *business solutions* using *applications* software. As such it was, more than anything else, an *applications system*. Because of the trend-setting technology it embodied, it also represented an *"advanced solution."* We thought the number 400 carried connotations having to do with the middle ground of computers. IBM's personal computers were designated by a single digit—the IBM PS/1, the IBM PS/2. Our mainframes went by four-digit names—the IBM 3080 or the IBM 3090. Three digits were right in between, as the computer itself was. At any rate we were happy to have the name—any name—because at that point we literally had to hold up printing manuals and such because we didn't know what to call our machine.

By June 1988, we were ready. Few times in IBM's long and illustrious history had a product been so well prepared to go out into the market. Nearly every conceivable factor affecting the AS/400's long-term success had been covered. The machine had tested out with flying colors. We were ready to fill orders from day one from three different plants around the world. With more than 2,500 applications ready to run on it, our customers could get down to business right away and with the software translated into 27 different national languages, there'd be no waiting by our esteemed customers outside the United States. Our sales force was primed and ready to go—with sales plans and strategies tailored to very deliberately targeted markets. Our Business Partners were ready to sell the machine, equipped and prepared with their own applications. Underpinned by trenchant positioning statements, we had strong advertising and public relations programs in place. We had contingencies for the inevitable competitive counter-punches to come. Our support and service engineers had been checked out on the new machine. The press and other opinion-makers had been prepared to give an accurate, and fair, assessment. It was, in a word, awesome.

Even with all this, we knew it wouldn't hurt to have some good luck too. On June 17, 1988, four days before we would unveil the AS/400 to the world, we received an omen —a good omen. Some sales representatives from our Sacramento office decided to take an outing to the nearby Cal-Expo Harness Racing track where, in the first race for two-year-old fillies, they found, ready for the running, horse number one—named Silver Lake. She was eight-to-one odds to win, but they couldn't resist betting on her. The starting bell clanged, the gates banged open, and Silver Lake bolted out with the pack. At the finish, though, it was Silver Lake, the winner!

The unveiling of the AS/400 was set for June 21, 1988. It just so happened we had picked the summer solstice, the longest day of the year. It was a good thing; we needed all the daylight we could get. Our product announcement followed the sun across the world. We started out in Japan, then Australia, and on to all the great capitals of Europe —Rome, Bonn, Paris, London, and others. In each locale we had a briefing and celebration. But the main event we reserved for New York City. We assembled more than 2,000 members of the press and guests in IBM's midtown Manhattan headquarters at 590 Madison Avenue. We arranged for the largest private telecast ever; the proceedings were going to be beamed to 100,000 customers and prospects gathered at IBM plants, branch offices, theaters, convention centers, and other sites around the globe.

A succession of IBM executives delivered addresses. Finally, the podium went to Terry Lautenbach, the head of IBM's U.S. operations. He gave a particularly feisty talk. What we were about to unveil, he said, proved that IBM was in the mid-range market to stay. What's more, it meant that IBM was going on the offensive. Not only that, but what the audience was about to see represented, he said, the fruits of a "new IBM"—one that was more reactive to its markets and one, most of all, that *listened* once again to its customers.

With that, amid a puff of smoke and the strains of the theme to *2001: A Space Odyssey*, the line of six AS/400 models rose on lifts from beneath the stage floor. For those of us who had toiled so long and hard to create a computer against almost impossible odds, it marked a defining moment. As the spotlights snapped onto the AS/400s illuminating their image into the minds of hundreds of thousands of people around the world, we were suddenly confronted, not just with what we had actually achieved in the form of a metal and silicon machine but with a realization—a realization that we had transformed ourselves into a different, stronger, and more effective enterprise.

While for us this stood as a breathtaking few seconds, this spectacle—this celebration of our machine—is not what left the day's most indelible stamp. Following this official debut, in New York and in IBM sales offices around the world, *customers and Business Partners offered testimonials to our machines.* Many were on hand to demonstrate their applications *at work.* We had invited them to take part because their contributions made the day theirs as much as ours. And what could have made for a more credible—more powerful—endorsement? We had users, with some detachment and objectivity, attesting to the machine's capability. Even better, among those giving demonstrations were software vendors who had changed their allegiances from competing machines to our own Silverlake, our AS/400.

We started taking orders immediately. In fact, one of our branch offices in Long Island held a contest to see which sales person could sell the most machines on announcement day. Chairman John Akers dashed to Rochester for a briefing by a Business Partner in Julie Furey's Solution Showcase and to take part in a special celebration we put on for those who had worked so hard on the Silverlake. It was, in short, quite a day.

Our launch was a spectacular success. For as high as expectations had mounted, we exceeded them. Sparkling reviews and positive press clipping in publications around the world began appearing by the scores. "Big Blue puts the bite back into its mid-range systems," one headline blared. IBM "has moved very quickly and nimbly," a consultant with International Data Corp., a computer market research firm, was quoted as saying. Even competitors conceded the formidability of what we had done. An official of Fujitsu, one of our Japanese competitors, was quoted as saying, "Frankly we hadn't thought of IBM as a serious contender for this segment before . . . . but we will surely be affected now." Perhaps our biggest compliment came from archrival DEC. In the introduction of the AS/400 "I saw the new IBM—responsive and aggressive," one ' of its executives wrote in the company's in-house *Digital News*.

Even Wall Street took notice. Within days of the announcement, IBM's stock shot up more than 10 points, solely on the strength of the AS/400's market introduction. Most significantly, however, sales took off. We hit our annual sales projections for Europe—13,000 machines—in just 60 days. Within four months, we had sold some 25,000 units, a number that exceeded the pace set by the fabulously successful IBM personal computer on its much celebrated introduction in 1981. The AS/400 stood as the most successful new computer introduction in IBM's entire 75-year history.

But we weren't about to recline on our kudos. We knew that four months, no matter how many good tidings they brought, amounted to nothing more than a blink in terms of the AS/400's planned lifespan of more than 10 years. We wanted the AS/400 line to be enduring. We knew things could still go awry, and that the AS/400 wasn't so entrenched that it could withstand a major reversal. We intended to do everything we possibly could to make certain we didn't suffer any setbacks. So we spent as much effort following up on the AS/400's launch as we did preparing for it. We had shaped many of the conditions for the machine's success thus far, and weren't going to cease our efforts to mold them some more.

When we received some negative publicity—there were about six articles we considered less than glowing—we had Bruce "Ask Bruce" Jawer, the engineer who was such a credible technical translator, call the writer or reporter, not to berate or bellyache but just to make sure they were looking at our machine with a well-informed understanding.

Our training efforts didn't let up either. Even though many of them had hands-on experience with the AS/400 during the Migration Invitational, we wanted to make sure that *all* our Business Partners understood the new machine. So they could provide the best sales and service support possible, we had them brought into Rochester for a week of training.

But if there was a pivotal factor in the long-term success of the AS/400, we knew it would come down to doing everything we possibly could to make certain our customers remained satisfied. If problems occurred—as they inevitably would—they had to be fixed, and fast. This wasn't just an intuitive notion on our part. We had seen surveys that proved it: In a sampling of new product buyers, 91 percent of those who never had a problem with a product would recommend it to someone else. But among those *who had a problem that was satisfactorily fixed* the recommendation rate ran even higher—94 percent.

We considered customer satisfaction of such paramount importance that we established a highly formalized process for resolving complaints. We already had a structure in place; Furey had set up a Customer Satisfaction Team as one of his earliest acts in transforming us into a market-driven enterprise. After we introduced the AS/400, however, we expanded the entire process for dealing with customer problems.

For the most part, problems were handled in the field through one of our branch offices. However, when a complaint went unresolved and moved up the chain to Furey, Schwartz, other executives—anyone—it was referred to our 15-person Customer Satisfaction Team. Once there, the complaint was assigned to a single member, who became the "detective" on the case. The caseworker's responsibility was to find out what went wrong and then resolve it. We didn't want an unhappy customer made all the more unhappy by getting lost in some faceless bureaucracy. We also set a deadline—every complaint must be fixed within 14 days. To make sure that they were, every pending case —we called them "crit sits" for "critical situations"—came

174

up for a review before Schwartz and his top managers at White Plains every two weeks.

We *empowered* the Customer Satisfaction Team to do whatever it took. They replaced hardware. They replaced software. In some cases, they replaced whole systems. In a few instances, they sent an entire team to a customer's computer site, even if it meant flying thousands of miles. In one such case, we found that the problem wasn't in our machine at all; the customer's computer kept suffering from electrical interferences because of an improperly grounded wiring system.

We decided it wasn't enough to wait for problems to turn up—*we actually decided to go out and find them*. Our proactiveness found its impetus in a rather insignificant incident. One of our executives had taken his teenage daughter's used Honda to a dealer for servicing. A few days later, to his astonishment, the dealership called just to make certain he was happy with the tune-up. He was so impressed, he suggested that we make a similar gesture to our customers. We agreed, and it didn't take much doing. We already had in place a telemarketing group whose job was to prospect businesses for sales leads. We tapped this 100-person group to make our follow-up calls. Ninety days after an AS/400 was shipped, our own AS/400 computers, using the advanced technology of telephony we had designed into the system, would automatically alert our telemarketing staff to call the customer. The computer would flash up onto to the terminal screen the customer's name, phone number, and other account specifics. When we phoned, we didn't go into anything too elaborate. "We just wanted to say, 'Thanks', and know how you were getting along with your computer," we told the customer. "If you have any complaints or suggestions, please tell us about them."

In the vast majority of cases all we did was impress already pleased customers. When we did receive a complaint we immediately referred it to the nearest IBM branch office. Then we asked the computer to alert us again so we could call back to make sure the complaint had been resolved. We tracked complaints carefully too. At the first sign of a negative trend, we immediately began looking back into the design and manufacturing process so we could correct any problems at the source.

In a few instances we actually made a pre-emptory strike at resolving a problem. For instance, we found that we'd given our sales representatives a bad directive. We told them that the smallest model in the AS/400 line would work with just four megabytes of internal memory when they were to run System/36 applications. But it really needed eight megabytes to function efficiently. We already had sold several machine with inadequate amounts of memory. But thanks to our follow-up calls we found out about the problem early—two weeks, in fact, before a meeting of COMMON, a 6,000-person independent group formed years ago by the users of our various IBM Rochester-made computers.

In another era, Furey would have unsuspectingly walked into that COMMON meeting, only to be caught unawares. He would have been publicly and embarrassingly skewered by peeved customers before an important group. Instead, he was ready and had worked on a solution with Bill Grabe. He marched into the meeting, told the group about the problem, how we intended to fix it, and then offered to give to customers—for free—the extra memory that they needed until we could find a way of making the machine work just as well with four megabytes of memory. The result: He received a standing ovation. The incident actually turned out to generate positive publicity. Because we had acted in anticipation, the headlines didn't highlight the problem. Instead, they highlighted our response, saying our efforts characterized what they described as "the new IBM."

Our efforts worked. In a survey released in February 1990, by the Sierra Group, a market research and consulting organization that checked in with customers of leading mid-range systems, the AS/400 placed first in hardware service, software support, and system performance with a satisfaction rating of 8.5 on a scale of 10. In the quality-conscious Japanese market, the Nikkei Computer

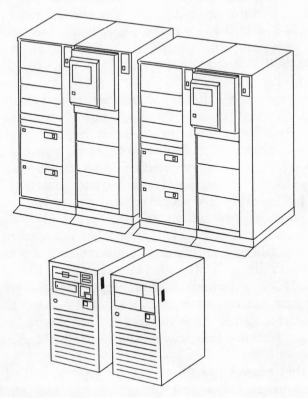

Figure 12. AS/400 family

Satisfaction Rating ranked the AS/400 small systems first and the AS/400 large systems third among thirteen different computers.

The biggest payoff of all our post-launch efforts, however, came in momentum. If anything, the AS/400's success gathered steam over time—within a year and half of its unveiling, we had sold 100,000 AS/400s around the world. They just weren't replacement machines either. Our installed base of IBM Rochester systems burgeoned to 450,000. Most of all, we went from being a "nice little business" for IBM to being a nice big one. After the launch, AS/400 sales grew at double-digit rates, even though overall growth in the entire mid-range market was languishing at around 4 percent annually. By the end of 1990, we had become a $14 billion business, enough to place us, had we been a company unto ourselves, in 28th place in the U.S. Fortune 500 1991 rankings, and 85th place in the global Fortune 500.

Our experience offered plenty for other companies in other industries to absorb. We showed that a product launch can't be a one-time event; it has to be seen as a process—a process that begins well before a product's introduction and continues well after. And the launch process also has a higher purpose, one beyond just making sure things go smoothly. By preparing early, you can help *shape your customers' perceptions* of your product. This allows *you*, not others, to position your product in terms of its perceived benefits and differences compared to the competition. By following up well after the launch, you can obtain valuable feedback, information that helps you to *continuously exceed your customers' expectations*. This, more than anything, distinguishes those companies that shape themselves into organizations that never stop learning and renewing themselves.

All this caused the AS/400 to be an unqualified success at its debut. But it wasn't enough. Along with making the AS/400 a standard-setting machine, we had vowed to make ourselves *the* model of a market-driven enterprise for all of IBM. We wanted IBM Rochester, as an ongoing concern, to stand out as the best of the best. But if we were to certify that we had fulfilled that lofty ambition, there was only one way to prove it. We had to put ourselves up against the toughest standards of business excellence. They were the standards established as part of *the* most prestigious and coveted recognition in American business—the Malcolm Baldrige National Quality Award.

10

WINNING
THE
BALDRIGE

Are we really world class?

—KEVIN L. ANDERSON, Manager of Engineering Strategy

The harder we tried, the more muddled we got. But they sat there—these five men before us—betraying no reaction. With no hint of whether we were giving them the right answers, we became more unsure with each question they asked. In desperation, we resorted to impressing them with the sheer weight of facts, which only made things worse. Then our replies began to degenerate into long-winded regurgitations. At moments, we felt like one of those ill-prepared law students berated and belittled at the crusty inquiries of John Houseman's tyrannical *Paper Chase* professor, Kingsfield.

It was September 1989—the surrounding cornfields were crowned with their yellow tassels—and we were undergoing an exhaustive three-day, on-site evaluation by five exam-

iners, all part of competing for the coveted Malcolm
Baldrige National Quality Award. By then, the AS/400 was
selling in numbers beyond our sunniest projections, our
revenues were on target to a second consecutive year of
double-digit growth, and, best of all, we were reclaiming
market share. But as good as all that was, it wasn't enough.
We were still out on the prairie, and, despite our accomplishments, had yet to shake our sod-buster image. But
winning the Baldrige—now that would prove beyond any
shadow of a doubt we were as sophisticated as any city-
slicker part of IBM.

The Baldrige was to us—to most of corporate America
for that matter—what the World Series was to the Oakland
Athletics and what the Oscar was to Dustin Hoffman and
The Rain Man that year. We saw it as the foremost recognition of excellence in business. The few companies who won
it vaulted to the very pinnacle of corporate prestige. Before
that day in September, we were hoping for the same thing.
But as our time before the examiners passed, we started
going on an emotional rollercoaster ride. We were up
—optimistic and hopeful about winning. And then we were
down, thinking less about winning and more about simply
getting through it all with our dignity intact.

The Baldrige competition was only two years old back
then, having been established in 1987 by an Act of Congress. It emerged from a national case of the jitters over
America's waning competitiveness, particularly vis-à-vis the
Japanese. By the mid-1980s, "Made in Japan" stood as the
mark of superior quality, and there was no doubt that the
island nation's reputation for quality had been one of the
main factors leading to its emergence as an economic
juggernaut. In dissecting its rise to competitive preemi-
nence, more than a few people noticed that Japan had its
own longstanding quality award, the Deming Prize (named,
ironically, after an American quality expert) held in esteem
higher than Mount Fuji. Like our Academy Awards night,
the Deming awards ceremony took place on prime-time TV.
The hope was that a similar award would help revive an
American passion for excellence too.

America's equivalent to the Deming took its name from Secretary of Commerce Malcolm Baldrige, an amateur cowboy who died in a rodeo accident in 1987. Despite its Congressional origins, the Baldrige isn't a government program—at least not exactly. Though overseen by the U.S. Commerce Department's National Institute of Standards and Technology, NIST (the old Bureau of Weights and Measures), it is co-administered by two quality trade associations and funded almost entirely by a $10 million endowment created from the contributions of private enterprise. It represents a unique effort at public-private cooperation. But its greatest virtue lies in something else—namely, what it has done to articulate a *concrete* standard of excellence readily applicable to modern business enterprises aspiring to world-class competitiveness.

Until the Baldrige came along, quality was largely one of those ephemeral subjects—like beauty in the eye of the beholder. It was easy enough for politicians and business leaders to pontificate about the need for more of it. To make it even more susceptible to vacuous platitudes, the whole idea of quality mutated during the 1980s and became much broader. No longer was quality just a matter of inspecting for scratches and dents, of seeing that the product simply worked when it went out the door. Instead, it became a code word for doing it right the first time. And "it" encompassed all the activities a firm engages in to produce and deliver a product or service. The bestselling *In Search of Excellence* was really a book about quality—about quality products and services sent into the marketplace by *quality* companies.

In Search of Excellence served up many wonderful anecdotes from successful companies and provided a subjective assessment of an evanescent standard—"excellence." Its intent was not to tell us in a methodical, comprehensive way what made them that way. America's growing concerns over quality begged other questions. What would it take to produce an undisputed, world-class standard of quality? What, in fact, was that standard? Could it be put in some measurable form? How could you tell how close you were to it and when you reached it?

181

The Baldrige has answered those questions. To win it, you must meet certain well-defined standards. And those standards have transformed the once elusive notion of "quality" into a *concrete, quantifiable, consensus* set of criteria. Contestants for the award are judged according to seven categories: leadership, information and analysis, quality planning, human resource utilization, quality assurance, quality results, and customer satisfaction. Each category is further subdivided into more than 100 items of consideration.

The Baldrige standards also represent an all-encompassing notion of quality. Its categories and their sub-items really address aspects of what the Baldrige describes as a "total management system." This includes everything from management leadership to employee involvement—all in addition to the more traditional quality concerns of assurance and customer satisfaction. So it's clear: To the Baldrige, quality is an end, and *everything* about the way you do business constitutes the means for getting there. To aspire to the Baldrige is really "the quest for excellence" —the very words that appear on the official Baldrige emblem.

We were heartened to know that our own vision of quality and excellence was consistent and compatible with the Baldrige standards. In fact, although we articulated them a little differently, we were holding ourselves to Baldrige-like aspirations of quality—aspirations of excellence—before the Baldrige was even a twinkle in Congress' eye. For example, the Baldrige category that weighs most heavily in the judging has to do with customer satisfaction. According to the Baldrige standards, delighted customers are the ultimate measure of quality. We believed the same thing. But we described it as being *market-driven*; put your customers above everything and then all else—market share, sales, profits, self-renewal—will follow. We knew that making customers delighted would demand more than delivering an innovative, reliable product. We also had to give them applications, distribution, and support and service. And to do that, we reexamined ourselves and the way we and our Business Partners operated—in *every way*.

We had to do things differently. We needed a leader, a vision, the right organization, far-reaching data and analysis, superior planning, a compressed development and manufacturing process, early defect prevention, customer involvement, an empowered work force, and a well-prepared product launch into target markets. All these together made for quality with a "Big Q," as we put it. They were the means to the end. They made for the success of the AS/400, for organizational excellence. And they made us, or so we felt, a contender for the Baldrige.

Our quest for the Baldrige began in the winter of 1988, the first year the award was offered. IBM had been a strong supporter of a national quality award and was among those companies to endow the program. IBM wanted to compete for the prize. The Baldrige competition is set up so that companies themselves can go after the award, or divisions or units of companies can enter. Competition takes place in three classes—manufacturing, services, and small business. IBM decided it would go after the award in the manufacturing division, of course, and that it would send a single one of its sites as a contender. To pick the part of IBM that would wear the Big Blue colors in the run for the Baldrige, our corporate quality executives decided to hold an internal competition.

Competing for the Baldrige is far more than an information-gathering task; it's a grueling self-analysis involving virtually every process and aspect of your business. In a 75-page application, you have to show how you meet the 100 or so Baldrige examination items. For a large operation such as ours—we had some $14 billion in worldwide system sales by then—collecting all that data and then boiling it down to its essence is an incredibly intense undertaking. We were asked to be one of five IBM sites to take a stab at becoming IBM's entry that year. We got the call in February, three weeks before the company wanted a Baldrige-like application from us and the other sites.

We were just months away from introducing the AS/400—coming down the last stretch of a two-year sprint toward completing the Silverlake Project. It was hardly the time for us to take on this kind of extracurricular activity but we agreed to give it a try. So we hastily assembled a task force led by Roy Bauer and, for the next 21 days, we dug, scratched, gathered, and patched together what we considered to be our quality story. Unfortunately, any sense of brevity abandoned us. By the time our deadline arrived, we wound up submitting a 10-inch thick tome—far too fat and, worse, far too nebulous, to be a credible entry.

As we expected, we were passed over. It only made sense. We were in the midst of a product transition, and that fact alone left us without the continuity of quality results we needed as a viable contender. Although our System/36 and System/38 machines had an industry-leading reputation for customer satisfaction, the AS/400 was, at that point, an untried machine. Plus, we simply didn't need the additional distraction at such a crucial time in the Silverlake Project's final stages. We accepted HQ's decision with equanimity and wished the site that was picked—IBM's manufacturing operation at Endicott, New York—the best of luck. By competing, however, we learned the value of the Baldrige assessment, we gained insight into our strengths and weaknesses, and we felt we had a good chance to win.

The Baldrige attracted 66 contestants by its May 1988 application deadline. Though the law creating the Baldrige authorizes as many as six recipients—two in each of the manufacturing, service, and small business classes—every year, only three applicants were deemed good enough to win it. These were Motorola Inc., the Commercial Nuclear Fuel Division of Westinghouse Electric Corp., and Globe Metallurgical Inc. of Cleveland, Ohio. By the time they received their Baldrige trophy—a beautiful Steuben crystal obelisk encasing a gold Baldrige medallion—at an official ceremony in the nation's capitol in December that year, the AS/400 was selling like hot cakes. Shortly after that, when it was time to decide who would represent IBM in the run for the 1989 Baldrige, we were the hands-down choice.

Tom Furey asked Bauer to head the effort once again. But Bauer declined. He'd switched to a newly created position in planning, and by then simply didn't want to compromise his work or the high-powered group he had just formed. We began preparing in December, well ahead of the May 1989 application deadline. We assigned each of the application's seven categories to its own author, who was someone in our line organizations, right from the trenches. Applying for the Baldrige is an exercise in self-assessment. Even if you never get close to winning the award, there's a virtue in comparing yourself to the world-class standards the Baldrige represents for the insights that self-analysis brings. Even though we'd put ourselves through the evaluation the year before, preparing the application still proved extraordinarily grueling.

The road to corporate excellence is never-ending. It's like chasing perfection; you get better, but you never really arrive. Achieving Baldrige-winning levels of quality is a journey, and the application serves as nothing more than a snapshot of where you happen to be along the way. We'd come a long way since the 10-inch-thick application we produced the year before. So despite all that work, we had to start from scratch when it came to creating 1989's application. And, you not only have to show what you do, you have to explain *how* you do it. The Baldrige is not only about quality results, it's also about quality *processes*, about organizational learning and continuous improvement. For some reason, our authors found it tough to tell our story in anything but anecdotal bits and pieces. What's more, the judging is so tough that no claim can be left unsubstantiated. Everything you say in the application must be authoritative; it has to be corroborated by data and fact.

But the biggest reason compiling our application proved so teeth-grinding was that the Baldrige requires that you explain how you do business *overall*. You're really submitting your "total management system" to judgment. And to do that you must understand how all the major facets of your business interface and interact. It's surprising how few people in large businesses below the chief executive level comprehend how a business functions *in its totality*. It's especially difficult to find that higher, conceptual level of understanding in a company as organized around various and separate functions as IBM. People tend to be very competent in their field; they know what they do well enough. But they often find themselves unable to step back to see how their work meshes with someone else's. It's really the old can't-see-the-forest-for-the-trees syndrome, and is one of the biggest afflictions standing in the way of a higher level of American quality and competitiveness.

As our Baldrige application came together that year, it was failing to provide that overall synthesis. Each of the seven sections constituted an individual chapter, but they lacked a certain connectedness that would have rendered them into a broad, seamless, and compelling account of our quality story. By February, it became clear that the application was in trouble. Our independent scoring team had given it a negative review. According to its evaluation, the application was so faulty it would score only 200 points or so out of the Baldrige's possible 1,000. To rescue the effort, Furey asked—no, insisted—that Bauer join the process. Bauer's role was to serve as coordinating architect. He established an overall theme and illustrated how the seven categories held together. Then he began pumping up the authors who had become so bogged down, lost, and demoralized by the immense task of distilling our story into its most essential, interrelated elements. Finally, he worked one on one with each of the seven authors during the next months of assessment.

After much kicking and gnashing—and not a little rewriting—we got our application boiled down to the 75-page maximum and out the door just in time to meet the deadline. For the next four months, it was out of our hands. Our story would have to speak for itself through the successive stages that characterize the Baldrige judging process.

Ours was one of 40 applications that year. Each was assigned a panel of six or so examiners, plucked from a pool of perhaps 300 or so quality experts—either from consultancies or companies—who volunteer each year to help with the judging process. NIST is scrupulous in making sure no conflicts of interest prevail. Examiners must have no ties, previous or present, to the companies connected with an application they are to review. The examiners rate each application on a cumulative point system that can go as high as 1,000, which stands for the achievement of world-class quality standards. Each of the seven categories making up the Baldrige application is worth a predetermined and varying number of points. Customer satisfaction, for example, counts as 30 percent of the scoring, more than any other category.

The applications deemed adequate to move ahead in the competition are put to a review by a *second* panel of examiners. They apply the same scoring process, and the field is winnowed yet again. At the point that it is eliminated from contention, every applicant receives a report from the Baldrige examiners, assessing their strengths and weaknesses. The feedback also tells them what they must do to reach world-class quality levels. We made it through this second examination and became one of 10 finalists. This entitled us to what is known as a "site-visit" by yet a third panel of Baldrige examiners. In short, they were coming to Rochester to see our operation for themselves.

The team of examiners arrived in late September. To make sure they weren't going to be influenced in any undue way, they declined our offer to pick them up at the airport—that's how squeaky clean they wanted this visit to be. There were five examiners—a consultant, a college professor, and three quality executives from companies. We started out on a Tuesday morning. They spent an hour introducing themselves and explaining the agenda they wanted to follow. Of course, we had no idea ahead of time what they wanted to see. We took them on a quick tour of our operations. Then the examination began in earnest.

The examiners have two purposes for these visits. The first is to obtain elaboration on any or all the information contained in the application. The second, and biggest, however, is to look for corroboration. It's one thing to talk quality—it's another to achieve it. The examiners want proof positive that you've actually done what you say you have. So they asked questions—piercing ones and lots of them. It's really not unlike defending a doctoral thesis.

Since we'd never been through a site visit before, we couldn't really prepare; the best we could do is organize our corroborating data. We filled five—*five*—five-drawer file cabinets with backup material. Then each one of our category authors filled up a three-inch ring binder with what they considered the most relevant information. We arrayed ourselves—about 15 of us counting authors and IBM Rochester executives and support people—in a room before the examiners. They started shooting their questions. Can we see minutes from your Rochester Management Board meetings? How did you generate these statistics? How does performance here compare to that of your competitors? Show us the numbers. How did you arrive at them? May we please talk to someone who is responsible for tracking the reliability of your computers? And so on.

That's when we began to feel like a room full of Kingsfield's hapless students. As our confidence began to erode, we began giving long-winded, unfocused answers, which created more questions, which caused our confidence and our responses to degrade more. We began confusing them and ourselves with too many facts, which begged more questions, which begged for more facts. We went on like this until 8 o'clock in the evening. The next day we went from 8 in the morning to 8 at night again. They got tired. We got tired. Although no one became overtly cranky, the body language spoke volumes about the degree of frustration filling the room—theirs and ours. It didn't take long to see the process start to go downhill.

They left. Despite how roughly the site visit went, our hopes of winning remained intact. As the weeks passed, the AS/400 continued to rack up stellar results in the market.

Then, finally, in October when they traditionally announced the Baldrige winners, we received the call. It came from Curt Reimann, associate director for quality programs who oversees the Baldrige Award at NIST. He didn't have to say anything more than his name, and we knew. The winners are told by the Secretary of Commerce. We'd lost. The word went out and a few of us cried. The one thing that would have put the Silverlake Project and our success beyond reproach eluded us again.

There were only two winners of the 1989 Baldrige Award—the Business Products and Systems division of Xerox Corporation and Milliken & Co., the textiles company from South Carolina. When we received the feedback from our on-site evaluation we learned why we hadn't joined them. Though we had requested one, IBM's corporate quality executive declined to be present for the site evaluation. His obvious absence led the judges to question IBM's overall commitment to quality. That hurt us. What's more, the Baldrige puts a big emphasis on quality trends, and a trend, according to the Baldrige criteria, is three to five years of results. Our trends for the AS/400 were barely a year old. That hurt us too. To make our case even weaker, we didn't do the best job of portraying our quality heritage going back to the System/36 and System/38.

But the biggest failing on our part involved our inability to adequately articulate just how all-encompassing our efforts had been. We were eloquent—if not on our feet at least in the written application—in describing our quality initiatives within our planning function, development lab, and in our manufacturing facilities. We were clear in expressing how we involved our customers. But we floundered when it came to depicting our efforts as they involved the sales and service side of our operations. Again, the Baldrige, in assessing a company's "quest for excellence," places a huge emphasis on a holistic approach to quality. We had, in fact, taken this very same holistic approach to the Silverlake Project. We'd made the marketing and sales functions an integral part of the AS/400's creation; we included them in the development process

189

earlier than ever before. But we didn't make that clear to the Baldrige examiners. The reason had more to do with perspective than anything else. We simply couldn't stand back far enough to fully grasp and then explain our enterprise as a totality. And that hurt us most of all.

The feedback report included other suggestions for improvement. It suggested we should work on quality processes for aspects of our enterprise that didn't directly relate to a product—aspects such as administrative and clerical services. And it suggested we could be stronger in non-product benchmarking. We went to work on addressing these issues right away. And then as the snow began to blanket the plains and 1990 approached, the question came up: After losing, would we go after the Baldrige again? We'd gotten a lot out of the process. If nothing else, the self-evaluation made it all worthwhile. We'd learned about some of our shortcomings—better yet, we fixed them. The success of the AS/400 just kept rolling along. But doing a critical self-assessment as required by the Baldrige takes an enormous amount of insight, time, and energy. Was it worth it to put ourselves through all that a third time? No matter how well it was doing, the AS/400 would have been on the market for less than two years by Baldrige 1990 deadline time—still not enough to establish a "trend" by Baldrige terms. We'd come close to winning in 1989; we knew that. The Baldrige people told us we finished in the very same point range as the winner. But we still wondered whether we should wait until 1992 when we'd be sure to have everything in place.

Opinions at IBM Rochester were pretty evenly split. But then we got a request we just couldn't refuse. IBM Chairman and CEO John Akers asked us to try one more time. In 1989, IBM had started giving out its own internal equivalent of the Baldrige. We won this first annual IBM quality award as the "best site" within the corporation. Given that and the roaring success of the AS/400, Akers figured that, even after falling short in 1989, we were still IBM's best bet to win the Baldrige. So it was set: We would try once again.

190

This time Bauer volunteered to lead the effort again. Despite his reluctance the year before, he knew we were just so close. Many other people who'd worked on the previous year's application also re-enlisted. But despite bringing all their experience to bear on it, compiling the application again turned out to be formidable. In just a year, we'd moved far enough along on our quality journey to make the previous year's application largely unusable. And the Baldrige guidelines got more stringent. To elevate our perspective—to look at ourselves more holistically—we asked the very top executives at our site to write the Baldrige application and they had the very same problem as our earlier authors. It took a real mind bend to convey the story as a process—to describe the "how" instead of just the "what" and "why." Larry Osterwise, the general manager of the IBM Rochester site, thought he'd have his section done in a weekend. He wound up investing 200 hours.

We did a few other things differently too. For each and every statement we made in the 75-page application, we created an evidence folder containing substantiating information to a particular claim. This way we were assembling our supporting documentation as we went along, rather than scrambling to bring it together if we received a site visit. Bauer also created a SWAT team of experienced assessment people who'd worked on the 1988 and 1989 applications, asking them to go over the processes described in the application with a fine-tooth comb. They helped add substantial refinements.

We submitted the application. It went through two evaluations and in August, we were informed that we had once again made it to the finals. We were going to get another site visit, scheduled for early September. And this time we were ready. We had our fact-folders gathered. We had agreed beforehand that we'd respond with succinct answers. And when the examiners asked a question pertaining to a particular section of our application, only the author of that section would respond with evidence-folder in hand, unless he or she referred the question to someone else for elaboration. We sent the lead examiners a background kit on our

operations at IBM Rochester, so we wouldn't have to waste
their face-to-face time with us on such basics. We also
mailed a special organization chart of IBM Rochester—one
that made it clear who did what and whom they could call
as an "expert witness" for a particular part of the application.

The examiners—six of them—arrived along with a representative from NIST. They introduced themselves and outlined their agenda. We gave them a tour. The questioning
began. And right from the start, it went without a hitch.
They asked for corroboration. We were right there with the
data and our explanations were crisp. During a site visit,
the examiners have their run of the place. When they heard
we had an IBM sales office in Rochester, they wanted to
visit it. They questioned the sales representatives there
about quality and our process linkages to them. The sales
reps answered as well as we could have. Then, on the spur
of the moment, they asked to visit the IBM sales office in
Minneapolis—80 miles away. They were greeted with answers proving that our quality efforts extended beyond the
walls of the development lab and manufacturing floor.

Things went so smoothly that the examiners finished up
a half day ahead of schedule. So they spent the remaining
time evaluating the various tools we used to measure
quality and then just walking around the site, holding
impromptu conversations with people they encountered. We
sent them off with cake and coffee. Unlike the year before,
we didn't part ways amid an air of fatigue and frustration.

A little more than a month later, on October 10, the call
came to Larry Osterwise. He, in turn, called Robert LaBant,
who, by 1990, had replaced Steve Schwartz as head of
IBM's mid-range computer group. It was October 10.
LaBant, along with the other top 20 executives of IBM,
including Akers, was closeted away in their semiannual
strategic planning conference. Because it is one of IBM's
most important gatherings, those attending are not to be
interrupted lightly. Osterwise had to cajole and threaten to
get his simple message—"Please call. Urgent"—into LaBant.
When LaBant received it, he was visibly distressed that

someone should dare to drag him from this meeting. Steve Schwartz, who by then had been named senior vice president of quality of all of IBM, was making a presentation.

LaBant left, talked to Osterwise, returned, and passed a note to Terry Lautenbach, the head of IBM's U.S. operations. Lautenbach passed the note to Akers. By this time, no one was listening to Schwartz anymore. Akers passed the note up to Schwartz, who until his change in assignments had led the IBM business group that included the Silverlake Project. No wonder Akers said, "It would be appropriate for you to read this to the group."

Schwartz glanced at the piece of paper and, as a huge grin crossed his face, he read its contents aloud. "IBM Rochester has just won the Malcolm Baldrige Award." At that, they stood up. These men, who constituted the chief council of IBM, one of the world's biggest corporations, rose to their feet—and broke into a spontaneous round of applause. It was so loud and so enthusiastic that, later, when we heard this story, many of us swore we could discern the faint echo of it all the way back in Rochester.

We celebrated the news that afternoon in Rochester, in a prototypically Midwestern manner. Not in the buttoned-down ways of the East Coast. Not in the laid-back style of the West Coast. No, we had an old-fashioned ice cream social in the cafeteria. There was a wonderful symmetry about gathering ourselves together in that cavernous room for the victory celebration. Here Furey had articulated his vision for us in the face of our abject skepticism; in this very room he told us we had it within ourselves to become *the* model for all of IBM. Now, in that same room, that vision had, finally and unimpeachably, reached its consummation.

Winning the award created a windfall of attention. We became the subject of literally hundreds of newspaper and magazine articles around the world. In December, we received the award itself in a ceremony at the White House hosted by President George Bush. "Most companies catch hell from the competition," the President said in making the award. "But these companies are in the lead because no

Figure 13. Baldrige Award trophy

competitor gave them a tougher time than they gave themselves." It was true. We had put ourselves through hell for two years through the Silverlake Project. But that day we were in heaven.

The Baldrige award went to IBM Rochester as a whole, and our winning came as the result of quality efforts that traced their roots back to as early as 1980. Nevertheless, it was in the development laboratory during the Silverlake Project that our transformation had really started. And much of what we'd done during the course of the Silverlake Project played a material, if not leading, role in capturing the Baldrige. Without our really knowing it at the time, the things we were doing fit neatly and precisely into the seven main Baldrige categories that served as earmarks of the "total management system" necessary for achieving our "quest for excellence."

Malcolm Baldrige Quality Categories

Management Principles	Leadership	Information & Analysis	Strategic Quality Planning	Human Resource Utilization	Quality Assurance	Quality Results	Customer Satisfaction
Visionary Leadership	●	◐	●	●	●	◐	●
Build a Team	●	○	◐	●	◐	◐	●
Segment, Target, Position	◐	●	●	◐	◐	●	●
Set & Manage Priorities	●	●	●	●	◐	◐	●
Break Time Barriers	●	◐	◐	●	◐	●	●
Form Partnerships	◐	○	●	●	●	●	●
Empower People & Groups	●	○	●	●	●	●	●
Set & Exceed Expectations	◐	●	●	○	◐	●	●
Form Cross-Functional Teams	●	◐	●	●	●	●	●
Research & Modeling	◐	●	●	○	●	●	◐

Degree of Correlation

○ Some   ◐ Medium   ● High

Figure 14. Correlation between AS/400 management principles and Baldrige's quality categories

The seven categories and the initiatives we took within the context of each were:

1. **Leadership.** We were in trouble in 1985. We needed a *leader* to help us see our way out of the predicament. Schwartz picked Tom Furey as that leader. Furey analyzed our situation. Out of what he saw there emerged a *vision*—that we could produce a standard-setting computer and, even more, that we could become *the* model of transformation for all of IBM. We were a product-driven

195

enterprise, too concerned with technology and our own purist ambitions, not the real needs of our customers. But Furey turned us about. He shaped us into a *market-driven* one. We put customer satisfaction above all else and, in so doing, came to address *all* the factors necessary for success in the marketplace.

He communicated his vision by giving it a careful articulation. He listened. He heard. He saw that he not only had to manage the problems of the moment but had to prepare for the future. He put the right people in the right places. He reorganized the lab into four tightly focused entities and established a cross-functional management group, the Rochester Management Board. He saw to it that his vision would live on and come to fruition, even beyond his own inevitable departure.

2. **Information and Analysis**. We asked two basic questions as we embarked on the Silverlake Project: Who are our customers? What do they want? We really couldn't answer. But we undertook an unprecedented effort to understand our customers and their needs. We used *research and modeling* to segment our markets by enterprise and location, industry, sub-industry, and size. Broken down this way, we were able to determine and then *target* our "natural" markets where we had existing strengths and "investment" markets where we needed to commit resources. Once we were able to see who are customers were—or would be—we could see what they needed in a machine.

We didn't relegate modeling to just our targeting and segmenting work. We used a *model* to make setting priorities much more methodical and objective; that allowed us to allocate resources in a much more systematic, holistic way. Instead of analyzing our competitors through a rear-view mirror to see what they had *done*, we started looking at where they were *going* by analyzing them as companies through every shard of information we could gather. Eventually, we compiled our market and competitive information into an electronic database. We made it accessible to managers on the site, elevating their perspective so they could see—and understand—the big picture of our operations, our strategy, and our market. After the AS/400 came to market, we made a "thank you" call to every customer 90 days after shipment. We asked for feedback. We used what they told us to *continuously exceed their expectations* by improving our machine and correcting problems, real and potential, at the source.

3. **Quality Planning**. Before the Silverlake Project, we just did product planning at IBM Rochester. That wasn't enough. Planning had to become a way of mapping out the future of the entire enterprise. With our *segmenting* analysis, we were able to *target* certain markets. From this we could plan a computer with characteristics that would appeal most to the markets we had chosen yet we knew we had to have more than a good computer. Success would depend on three other factors—applications, distribution, and support and service.

We were able to elevate the decision making that went into *allocating resources* to a much more systematic level by *setting priorities* for markets, technologies, and our System Plan, which embodied all our specifications for the Silverlake. We *shaped our customers' expectations* by meticulously planning for the Silverlake's introduction a year *before* it hit the market. We *formed partnerships with outsiders*. These included customers and Business Partners who helped validate our plans from their perspective. We also trained Business Partners and our field service engineers. We used our segmenting and targeting analysis to map out the *positioning* of the AS/400 so that it would be differentiated from its competition. We used our targeting plans and positioning statement

197

to develop sales programs tailor-made for the markets we wanted to pursue.

4. **Human Resource Utilization.** To get the Silverlake project finished in half the time, we had to win the hearts and minds of the 8,000 employees at IBM Rochester. We fostered buy-in through lots of communication, including all-employee meetings and Furey's continuing series of roundtables. But most of all, we did it by *empowering* our work force. We wanted them to be as self-managed as possible. Our managers were overworked. Our technical professionals, at the same time, were underutilized. So we had to get our managers to delegate responsibility and authority. We did that by establishing a specific set of expectations for each and every job in the development lab. With this tool, managers could gauge what they had to give up in terms of responsibility. Employees used it to understand what responsibilities they had to accept and what management expectations were.

We put into place a management development structure that would help foster *leadership*. Leaders point people in the right direction, then step out of the way to let others get the job done. We gave non-managers ownership in their part of the Silverlake Project. We set broad specifications for the computer, but *they* set the more specific objectives of performance, cost, quality, and completion date for their parts of the project. We also supplied people with the resources, mainly in terms of skills and knowledge, to enable them to get their jobs done. We provided education. We encouraged innovation and technical vitality. We made it easier for our technical professionals to apply for patents, and gave them incentives to publish papers and books. We helped nurture a *market-driven* perspective among our people by making them work with customers almost on a daily basis as part of their job.

5. **Quality Assurance**. To get the Silverlake out on time, we had to *break time barriers* and compress the development process. So instead of doing things so sequentially, we had to overlap. We developed the hardware in *parallel* with the software. But to do that, we had to *get it right the first time*. We started concentrating on removing flaws from the Silverlake in the design phase or as early in the development process as possible. We used new leading-edge technology, such as computer system simulation—a *model*—to test the Silverlake hardware design for flaws before a machine was ever actually built. On a daily basis, we tracked our progress toward writing 7 million lines of software code, not only for productivity, but for quality. If one of our modules looked as if it were in trouble, we had the Bug Stompers team of software programmers ready and waiting to come to the rescue.

To see that our plans stayed on track, we put special organizational structures *in place and staffed them with the right people*. In many cases, we created *cross-functional teams*. Jim Coraza's Project Management Team saw to the worldwide coordination of development and manufacturing. Schwartz and Grabe's Executive Steering Committee supervised the worldwide preparation of marketing and sales. To verify that the Silverlake would work the way we said it would, we sent 4,755 computer systems out to customers months before introduction. This early-ship program allowed us to test the AS/400 under live conditions.

6. **Quality Results**. The results of all these efforts were nothing short of spectacular. The AS/400 jumped off to faster sales than even IBM's enormously successful personal computer. We sold 100,000 units within 18 months. We were growing at double-digit rates. We regained market share and enjoyed double-digit sales growth. We became the benchmark for competing ma-

chines. In terms of traditional measures of product quality, we were a smash hit too. Of course, we developed the computer in 28 months, half the time it normally took. Because of our emphasis on *getting it right the first time,* we reduced engineering changes by 45 percent. We curtailed scrap and rework by 55 percent. System reliability surpassed that of the System/36 and System/38. We reduced delivery times from 3.5 months to just two weeks.

7. **Customer Satisfaction**. Of course, *everything* we did was ultimately aimed at pleasing our customers. Our *market-driven* philosophy imbued all of IBM Rochester with a customer satisfaction ethic. But we took several customer-satisfaction initiatives that were notably innovative. We involved *customers as outside partners* in the development process to an unprecedented degree, especially for traditionally guarded IBM. We had a prototype machine in a customer's shop seven months after development began. We created councils of customers and Business Partners. We openly told them about the Silverlake Project. We asked for their reactions and suggestions. We listened. We heard. We acted on what they said—months before Silverlake hit the market.

Even before the Silverlake was off the drawing board, we established a customer satisfaction team. They were empowered to do just about anything to make sure that customer complaints were resolved. We began a practice of calling our customers 90 days after they received their AS/400. The purpose was just to say "Thank you." But we also gathered valuable information that allowed us to make the AS/400 even better as time went on and to *continuously exceed customer expectations.*

From this it was clear that we had actually been working to win the Baldrige for years—before the Silverlake Project was barely underway and, certainly, before the Baldrige ever came into being. Once we took home the

Baldrige, IBM Rochester became the subject of much attention and scrutiny. We were featured in dozens of articles. We talked before the representatives of hundreds of associations and companies all around the world about our Baldrige-winning story. We played host to nearly a 1,000 companies who came to see how we work. We became an example to corporate America. All this didn't happen because we did things piecemeal. When it comes right down to it, we transformed ourselves—*and we did that by comprehensively instituting 10 management principles across the board*. We imbued these Silverlake principles—all of them —in everything we did, from beginning to end. And that, above all else, is what makes telling our story to others worthwhile. The virtue in our parable is this: It's not just about concepts. It's about implementing those concepts in a real-life situation that renewed an entire organization.

Because of that, we have become something of an example, an example to IBM and all American business. Chairman John Akers took to calling us the company's "rabbit." We had become the quick creature that had dashed out ahead of the rest of the company—the one the rest of IBM was destined to chase on the way to its own transformation. Indeed, IBM had begun embracing the market-driven model in a big way. It started adopting as standard operating procedures many of the things we did, including global segmentation analysis, partnership with customers and business associates, processes for breaking time barriers, and customer satisfaction calls. In many ways, IBM Rochester's struggle is representative of the challenges facing American business. Since the early 1980s, companies all across the country have been contending against intense global competition, yet they have been straining against the inertia of their own entrenched ways of doing things. It remains to be seen whether they will overcome these forces soon and whether they can transform themselves into winners.

But we are hopeful and optimistic. After all, we were in trouble once too. And we weren't given much of a chance of completing the Silverlake on time. But we did, and went on to become a Malcolm Baldrige winner and a model for others to boot. But we are not complacent; we have learned that "no matter how well we think we do something, we know it can be done better." In becoming an exemplar, we were proud, elated, and flattered. And, we have to admit, we were a little amused too. Even for us, it's hard to believe it all began in a cornfield on the prairie's edge in a Minnesota town.

BIBLIOGRAPHY

Suggested Reading

CHAPTER 1. CORPORATE TRANSFORMATION IN A CORNFIELD

H. W. Hogson, *Rochester: City of the Prairie*, Windsor Publications, Inc. 1989.
- History of the city of Rochester. Chapter 4 provides a brief description how IBM got there.

T. J. Watson Jr., *Father Son & Co: My Life at IBM and Beyond*, Bantam Books, 1990.
- Very readable and candid account by the son of the founder of IBM. Chronicles IBM's early years, the creation of its unique management system, and how it became the world's leading computer company.

T. J. Watson Jr., *A Business and Its Beliefs: The Ideas That Helped Build IBM*, McGraw-Hill Book Company, Inc. 1963.
- Columbia Business School lectures on the fundamental IBM management principles and their rationale. A must for anyone who wishes to understand IBM's culture.

F. G. "Buck" Rodgers, *The IBM Way: Insights into the World's Most Successful Marketing Organization*, Harper & Row, 1986.
- Memoirs from a top IBM sales executive, now retired.

F. M. Fisher, J. W. McKie, R. B. Mancke, *IBM and the US Data Processing Industry: An Economic History*, Praeger Publishers, 1983.
- A history of IBM and the industry in the U.S. from an economic perspective. Not light reading.

D. Andrews, J. Martin, T. Elms, D. Simeone, *The AS/400 Revolution: Guide to the AS/400 and IBM Strategy*, ADM, Inc., Connecticut, 1989.
- An outsider's perspective on IBM Rochester and the AS/400. Has readable chapters on the technical capabilities of the system. Speculates on IBM's future plans.

D. B. Yoffie, A. E. Pearson, "The Transformation of IBM," *Harvard Business School, Case Study N9-391-073*, Harvard Business School Publishing Division, June 27, 1991.
* Discusses how IBM is transforming itself under the direction of its chairman and CEO John Akers.

CHAPTER 2. LEADERSHIP AND VISION

N. M. Tichy, M. A. Devanna, *The Transformational Leader*, J. Wiley & Sons, 1986.
* Excellent study of the dynamics and processes that affect organizational transformation. Notable analyses on the pitfalls and inhibitors to change.

W. Bennis, B. Nanus, *Leaders: The Strategies for Taking Charge*, Perennial Library, Harper & Row, 1985.
* Cogent analysis on the difference between managing and leading. Asserts that shaping vision and enabling people and organizations to achieve extraordinary things are the hallmarks of leadership.

W. Bennis, *On Becoming a Leader*, Addison Wesley Publishing Co, 1989.
* Argues that leadership is an acquired attribute and describes how to acquire it.

J. M. Konzes, B. Z. Posner, *The Leadership Challenge*, Jossey-Bass Publishers, 1990.
* Another excellent study of the role of visionary leadership. Notable are not only the analysis but the blueprints offered for implementation.

T. J. Peters, *Thriving on Chaos: Handbook for a Management Revolution*, Alfred A. Knopf, 1988.
* Detailed and concrete exposition of management principles in an environment of intense competition, where innovation is a must. Prescriptions are useful and practical.

R. Moss Kanter, *The Change Masters: Innovation & Entrepreneurship in the American Corporation*, Simon & Shuster, 1983.
* How to recognize a stifling organization. How to create one that can change and innovate.

G. Hamel, C. K. Prahalad, "Strategic Intent," *Harvard Business Review*, May-June 1989.
* Strategic intent is the articulation of a leader's vision. Strategy is the continuous operational expression of that intent, which gives it direction, purpose, and meaning.

K. Labich, "The Seven Keys to Business Leadership," *Fortune*, October 24, 1988.
* Article identifies seven important characteristics of leaders with examples from corporate America. Empowerment and vision are the two most important.

CHAPTER 3. PUTTING PEOPLE IN PLACE

J. Benedetti, "A Talk with Tom Furey," *Systems 3X World*, September 1988.
* Interview on the state of IBM Rochester's business, the management team, and future plans for the product and customer applications.

D. C. Hambrick, "The Top Management Team: Key to Strategic Success," *California Management Review*, Volume 30, No. 1, Fall 1987.
* Paper argues that "team qualities are the essential foundation for a successful strategic process within the firm." Proposes and discusses the dimensions of those qualities.

P. F. Drucker, *Managing in Turbulent Times*, Harper & Row, 1980.
* One of the first management thinkers to recognize the dynamics of environmental change. Still applicable. Chapter 2 discusses the need to manage in two time-frames.

N. Tichy, R. Charan, "Speed, Simplicity, Self-Confidence: An Interview with Jack Welch," *Harvard Business Review*, September-October 1989.
* Describes Jack Welch's approach to organizational design and his preferred no-nonsense management style.

M. J. Stahl, G. M. Bounds, *Competing Globally Through Customer Value*, Quorum Books, 1991.
* Authors submit that companies need to structure themselves around net customer value—what they receive minus what they sacrifice. An analytic model is offered to measure and produce customer value.

G. Hamel, C. K. Prahalad, "Corporate Imagination and Expeditionary Marketing," *Harvard Business Review*, July-August 1991.
* The banner heading summarizes the paper well. "To realize the potential that core competencies create, management needs the imagination to envision markets that do not yet exist."

A. Cutaia, *Technology Projection Modeling of Future Computer Systems*, Prentice-Hall, 1990.
* Author identifies potential customer applications that are intractable in the current technology, but feasible with new technology. Technical book that projects the use and structure of future systems.

V. Tang, "ISDN, New Vistas in Information Processing," *IEEE Communications*, Volume 24, No. 11, November 1986.
* Paper projects customers' use of data processing evolving to the next stage of capability—information processing where sound and images play a major role.

J. B. Quinn, "Technological Innovation, Entrepreneurship, and Strategy," *Sloan Management Review*, Spring 1979.
* Identifies the inhibitors to innovation in large firms. More notably, specifies prescriptions to overcome them.

M. Tushman, D. Nadler, "Organizing for Innovation," *California Management Review*, Volume 28, Spring 1986.
* Major considerations for creating structures and climate that promotes innovation.

M. A. Maidique, R. H. Hayes, "The Art of High-Technology Management," *Sloan Management Review*, 1984.
* Describes the management characteristics of successful high-technology firms.

CHAPTER 4. GETTING TO KNOW OUR CUSTOMERS

P. Kotler, *Marketing Management, Analysis, Planning and Control*, Prentice-Hall, 1980.
* The definitive text on the subject. A must reading for those who wish to understand this discipline. Provides a very lucid exposition on market segmentation and targeting.

Y. J. Wind, R. J. Thomas, "Segmenting Industrial Markets," unpublished paper, Wharton School, University of Pennsylvania, 1991.
• Discusses the managerial decisions and processes for segmenting industrial markets.

Y. J. Wind, "Positioning Analysis and Strategy," in *The Interface of Marketing and Strategy*, JAI Press Inc., 1988.
• Discusses the concept of positioning and strategies for developing an effective one.

A. Ries, J. Trout, *Positioning: The Battle for Your Mind*, McGraw-Hill, 1981.
• A street-smart, practical approach to the notion that positioning is the new way to communicate in an overcommunicated society. Useful and fun to read.

T. DeMarco, *Structured Analysis and System Specification*, Prentice-Hall, 1978.
• A process-oriented approach to product planning. Begin with what the system should do (customer environment), and then how the system should work (technology and system design).

K. Ohmae, *The Mind of a Strategist*, McGraw-Hill, 1982.
• Focuses on the substance of strategy. Provides an excellent methodical approach to identify critical issues in the formulation of strategies.

M. E. Porter, *Competitive Strategy: Techniques for Analyzing Industries and Competitors*, The Free Press, 1980.
• Addresses the structure of an industry and competition. Within that structure forces are at play, and competitive strategies can be formulated. Very useful analytic tool.

M. E. Porter, *Competitive Advantage: Creating and Sustaining Superior Performance*, The Free Press, 1985.
• Develops the value-chain as a pivotal element in the formulation of competitive strategies.

D. L. Birch, *Job Creation in America: How Our Smallest Companies Put the Most People to Work*, The Free Press, 1987.
• Dramatic findings that small enterprises and not large corporations are the force that drive our economy.

D. K. Clifford Jr., R. E. Cavanagh, *The Winning Performance: How America's Mid-size Companies Succeed*, Bantam Books, 1985.
• Convincing analyses that show that mid-size companies outpace large companies in growth, profits, and other financial measures.

"The Stateless Corporation," *Business Week*, May 14, 1990.
* How companies are erasing national boundaries and becoming global with a local touch simultaneously.

K. Ohmae, *The Borderless World*, Harper Business, 1990.
* Thoughtful book about competing in global markets and becoming an effective global business.

The European Challenge 1992: *The Benefits of a Single Market*, Wildwood House England, 1988.
* Superb overview of the economic opportunities of Europe 1992 and the reasons why.

R. Hofheinz Jr., K. E. Calder, *The Eastasia Edge*, Basic Books Inc., 1984.
* Analysis and exposition on the surge of economic power, exports, and technology in the Pacific rim.

CHAPTER 5. ALLOCATING RESOURCES BY SETTING PRIORITIES

M. Schrage, "When Innovation Leads Corporations Away from Their Strategic Interests," *The Washington Post*, May 31, 1991.
* Points out the difficulty of killing projects. Correctly concludes that a multitude of unfocused efforts are more debilitating than effective.

"I Can't Work This Thing," *Business Week*, April 29, 1991.
* The result of mindless differentiation. "Poorly designed machines with unwanted features are driving consumers crazy." Provide only features that are needed.

T. L. Saaty, *Decision Making for Leaders*, University of Pittsburgh, 1988.
* A very readable presentation of the Analytical Hierarchy Process (AHP) with numerous examples illustrating its wide applicability.

T. L. Saaty, K. P. Kearns, *Analytical Planning: The Organizations of Systems*, Pergamon Press, 1985.
* Proposes a new conceptual framework for planning and identifies a methodological tool for integrating the concepts of systems and planning. Great discussion of the shortcomings of traditional approaches to planning.

T. L. Saaty, L. L. Vargas, *The Logic of Priorities: Applications in Business, Energy, Health and Transportation*, Kluwer Nijhoff Publishing, 1982.
* A more detailed and technical exposition of AHP with examples.

R. N. Cardozo, Y. Wind, "Risk Return Approach to Product Portfolio Strategy," *Long Range Planning*, 1985.
* The article describes how a risk-return portfolio analysis can be applied to product investment decisions.

D. A. Cowan, "Developing a Process Model of Problem Recognition," *Academy of Management Review*, Volume 11, 1986.
* Presents a theoretical model that explains how individuals recognize problems in organizational situations.

J. F. Rockart, D. W. DeLong, *Executive Support Systems: The Emergence of Top Management Computer Use*, Dow Jones Irwin, 1988.
* Describes computer usage by senior management. Addresses the problems of managing data, the organizational dynamics of usage and the linkages to business objectives.

V. Tang, "Executive Information System & Organizational Effectiveness: A Case Study," in press for *Journal of Systems Management*, 1992.
* Describes the role of an executive information system in improving organizational effectiveness. Paper analyzes potential inhibitors to success.

CHAPTER 6. BREAKING TIME BARRIERS

R. A Sulak, R. J. Lindner, D. N. Dietz, "A New Development Rhythm for the AS/400," *IBM Journal of Research and Development*, Volume 28, No. 3, 1989.
* A technical but highly readable exposition of the new development process used to dramatically reduce development cycle time.

Advantage AS/400: Application System/400 Technology, IBM Corporation, Publication No. SA21-9540-0.
* Over two dozen articles on the hardware, software and manufacturing technology of the IBM AS/400. Requires some technical background.

G. Stalk Jr., T. M. Hout, *Competing Against Time*, The Free Press, 1990.
* The book describes time as a new competitive dimension. It also outlines approaches on how to become a responsive company.

B. Dumaine, "How Managers Can Succeed Through Speed," *Fortune*, February 1989.
* How to gain a competitive advantage by getting there first.

H. Takeuchi, I. Nonaka, "The New Product Development Game," *Harvard Business Review*, January-February 1986.
* An example of how the Japanese shorten development cycle time and maximize learning from the market.

R. H. Hayes, S. C. Wheelwright, K. B. Clark, *Dynamic Manufacturing, Creating the Learning Organization*, The Free Press, 1988.
* Authors focus on the infrastructure issues for competitive advantage. Chapters 10 and 11 are particularly applicable to the issues of flexibility and development cycle time.

P. Bolwijn, T. Kumpe, "Manufacturing in the 1990's: Productivity, Flexibility and Innovation," *Long Range Planning*, August 1990.
* Authors identify four stages of competitive evolution: efficiency, quality, flexibility, and innovation. The battleground for the 1990s will be innovation.

P. R. Thomas, *Competitiveness Through Total Cycle Time: An Overview for CEO's*, McGraw-Hill Publishing Company, 1990.
* Shows that 60 to 90 percent of cycle time improvement can occur outside of manufacturing.

P. R. Thomas, *Getting Competitive: Middle Managers and the Cycle Time Ethic*, McGraw-Hill Publishing Company, 1991.
* Takes a middle manager's perspective and uses a pedagogical case study approach.

M. A. Meth, "Concurrent Engineering-Changing the Process for Bringing Products to Market," *Computer*, September 1991.
* Although published in a computer journal, the paper discusses general principles that help reduce cycle time.

Y. J. Wind, *Product Policy, Concepts, Methods and Strategy*, Addison Wesley, 1982.
* Comprehensive textbook. Covers the ground from market research, product planning, to development processes.

G. Hamel, C. K. Prahalad, "Corporate Imagination and Expeditionary Marketing," *Harvard Business Review*, July-August 1991.
* Expeditionary marketing—market research by introduction of new products.

P. E. Green, Y. J. Wind, "New Ways to Measure Consumer Judgements," *Harvard Business Review*, July-August, 1975.
- Highly readable article on the technique of conjoint analysis to determine consumer preferences for product or service features.

CHAPTER 7. FORGING OUTSIDE PARTNERSHIPS

B. J. Pine II, "Design, Test, and Validation of the Application System/400 Through Early User Involvement," *IBM Journal of Research and Development*, Volume 28, No. 3, 1989.
- Thorough and readable account of the processes where customers, business partners, and cross-functional teams were used to achieve time breakthroughs.

E. vonHippel, *The Sources of Innovation*, Oxford University Press, 1988.
- Seminal study that convincingly demonstrates that innovation occurs most frequently outside the firm among users and suppliers.

"King Customer," *Business Week*, March 12, 1991.
- In the final analysis, listening to customers and putting them first will improve profitability.

E. M. Rogers, *Diffusion of Innovations*, The Free Press, 1983.
- Pioneering work on the factors that influence the acceptance of innovations. Shows that communications and information exchange among major stakeholders will accelerate diffusion.

T. Baer, "IBM and Its Business Partners Piece the CIM Puzzle Together," Supplement to *Managing Automation*, May 1991.
- How IBM forms business partnerships in the industrial sector. Good sidebar on what is an "IBM Business Partner."

"Partners in Growth," Supplement to *Inbound/Outbound*, June 1990.
- Articles on new voice-applications developed by IBM business partners. A notable feature is how they describe the competitive advantages their customers can accrue.

J. R. Hauser, D. Clausing, "The House of Quality," *Harvard Business Review*, May-June 1988.
- Effective technique to link customer requirements with product features and thereby achieve quality.

M. E. Porter, *Competitive Advantage: Creating and Sustaining Superior Performance*, The Free Press, 1985.
* Analysis of suppliers and customers helps determine whom to cooperate with to gain a strategic advantage.

M. E. Porter, *Competitive Advantage: Creating and Sustaining Superior Performance*, The Free Press, 1985.
* Analysis of industry participants' position in the value chain provides insight on strengths and weaknesses.

J. L. Badaracco, Jr., *The Knowledge Link: How Firms Compete Through Strategic Alliances*, Harvard Business School, 1991.
* Theme is that intellectual capital is the critical element in forging business relationships.

CHAPTER 8. EMPOWERING PEOPLE

K. Labich, "The Seven Keys to Business Leadership," *Fortune*, October 24, 1988.
* Survey of CEOs identifies empowerment as the key to a successful executive.

T. J. Peters, *Thriving on Chaos: Handbook for a Management Revolution*, Alfred A. Knopf, 1988.
* Chapter on empowering people is particularly useful.

W. Bennis, B. Nanus, *Leaders: The Strategies for Taking Charge*, Perennial Library, Harper & Row, 1985.
* Another useful chapter on leadership and empowerment.

J. M. Konzes, B. Z. Posner, *The Leadership Challenge*, Jossey-Bass Publishers, 1990.
* Part four of the book addresses the subject of enabling people to act.

R. Charan, "How Networks Make Organizations Boundaryless—and Deliver Superior Results," *Harvard Business Review*, September-October 1991.
* To close the gap between CEO vision and superior execution requires a "new organizational biology." Thoughtful and thought provoking.

B. Dumaine, "Who Needs a Boss?," *Fortune*, May 7, 1990.
* Describes the successful practice of some companies where empowerment has boosted productivity dramatically.

B. Dumaine, "Bureaucracy Busters," *Fortune*, June 17, 1991.
* Groups of teams, projects, and alliances increase productivity and creativity.

P. F. Drucker, "Management and the World's Work," *Harvard Business Review*, September-October 1988.
* Makes the point cogently that management's job is to enable people to work together to amplify their strengths.

P. F. Drucker, *The New Realities*, Harper & Row, 1989.
* Drucker further elaborates on organizations whose composition is principally knowledge workers where the job of management is similar to that of a conductor of a symphony orchestra.

CHAPTER 9. REINVENTING THE LAUNCH

V. Tang, E. Collar, "A New Launch Paradigm: Case of the IBM AS/400," *Long Range Planning*, in press for publication in 1992.
* The paper rejects the notion that launching a new product is a one-time event in a linear sequential process. Rather, it should be part of a closed loop process.

J. Wind, V. Mahajan, "Marketing Hype: A New Perspective for New Product Research and Introduction," *Journal Product Innovation Management*, 4(1), March 1987.
* Paper argues that all stakeholders must participate in creating the market conditions for successful product launching.

M. E. Porter, *Competitive Advantage: Creating and Sustaining Superior Performance*, The Free Press, 1985.
* Analysis of industry participants' relative position in the value chain provides insight on critical partnerships required to sustain launch momentum.

V. Zeithaml, A. Parsuraman, L. L. Berry, *Delivering Quality Service: Balancing Customer Perceptions and Expectations*, The Free Press, 1990.
* Book describes the importance of meeting customer's expectations to generate customer satisfaction. Inference is that the management of expectations is therefore critical.

N. Percy, N. Morgan, "Internal Marketing: The Missing Half of the Marketing Program," *Long Range Planning*, April 1991.
* Emphasizes the application of the marketing discipline internally to improve marketing effectiveness.

CHAPTER 10. WINNING THE BALDRIGE

R. A. Bauer, *IBM Rochester Malcolm Baldrige Quality Lectures*, Unpublished, 1991.
* Lectures on the quality initiatives and practices in IBM Rochester that helped to win the Baldrige award.

1991 Application Guidelines, Malcolm Baldrige National Quality Award, United States Department of Commerce, National Institute of Standards and Technology.
* Describes the criteria used for the award examination and scoring. Summaries of the 1991 winners are descriptive and insightful.

"Commitment to Quality," *Electronic Business*, October 15, 1990.
* Special issue devoted to quality and the Malcolm Baldrige National Quality Award. Two special reports on the quality initiatives in IBM and IBM Rochester.

T. J. Peters, R. H. Waterman Jr., *In Search of Excellence, Lessons from America's Best-Run Companies*, Harper & Row, 1982.
* The original classic on the best practices from the most successful American companies. Book redefined the meaning of excellence in the context of American business.

R. D. Buzzell, B. T. Gale, *The PIMS Principles: Linking Strategy to Performance*, The Free Press, 1987.
* From substantial empirical evidence, the research establishes the value of quality.

M. Walton, *The Deming Management Method*, Perigee Books, 1986.
* Book identifies and describes fourteen key management practices and seven deadly diseases of management. Part two presents corporate examples.

K. Ishikawa, *What Is Total Quality Control*, Prentice-Hall, 1985.
* A Japanese approach to the subject.

P. B. Crosby, *Quality Is Free*, McGraw-Hill, 1979.
* Perspectives are that lack of quality is costly and having quality pays.

J. M. Juran, *Quality Control Handbook*, McGraw-Hill, 1962.
* Another American guru on quality.

"The Quality Imperative," *Business Week*, October 25, 1991.
* Comprehensive special issue covering quality in management, manufacturing, services, the public sector, and R&D.

Index

Index

Index